DISCONNECTING PARTIES

Managing the Bell System Break-Up: An Inside View

By

W. Brooke Tunstall

Corporate Vice President
Organization and Management Systems
AT&T

Foreword by
RICHARD TANNER PASCALE

Coauthor of *The Art of Japanese Management*
and Professor of Business Administration
Stanford Graduate School of Business
Palo Alto, California

McGraw-Hill Book Company

New York   St. Louis   San Francisco   Auckland   Bogotá   Hamburg
Johannesburg   London   Madrid   Mexico   Montreal   New Delhi
Panama   Paris   São Paulo   Singapore   Sydney   Tokyo   Toronto

Library of Congress Cataloging in Publication Data

Tunstall, W. Brooke.
    Disconnecting parties.

    Includes index.
    1.American Telephone and Telegraph Company.
I.Title.
HE8846.A55T86   1985   384.6′065′73   84-23338
ISBN   0-07-065434-4

1234567890   DOC/DOC   8987654

ISBN 0-07-065434-4

The editors for this book were William A. Sabin and Barbara B.
Toniolo, the designer was Mark E. Safran, and the production
supervisor was Thomas G. Kowalczyk. It was set in ITC Garamond
Light by University Graphics, Inc.

Printed and bound by R. R. Donnelley & Sons Company

This volume is dedicated to the tens of thousands of Bell System employees who responded so admirably to the enormous task of dismantling the enterprise that they had helped to build and sustain and that they had served so well. I only regret that space will not permit the special tributes that could be paid to so many organizations and individuals for the extraordinary nature of their contributions.

Contents

Foreword

During 1982 and 1983, those of us who earn our livelihoods endeavoring to advance the practice of management had to content ourselves with sideline perspectives on the epic corporate drama then unfolding within AT&T.

From the outside we could, of course, track the main events of the government's suit leading to the divestiture agreement. And due in no small part to excellent reporting in the nation's media, we could follow the manifold financial, organizational, and marketplace consequences flowing from the accord.

What we did not have were any real insights as to how divestiture, in all its daunting complexity, was being planned and organized, or how it might ever be managed in so short a period under such extreme pressures.

Now, with Brooke Tunstall's fine account, we at last have a firsthand perspective—a highly readable chronicle of the management of divestiture. *Disconnecting Parties* provides an insider's viewpoint on events that will be of intense interest to the management community: the planning and execution of the break-up, the vast corporate restructuring, the impact of events on a historic corporate culture, the lessons to be learned.

But beyond the management audience, I suspect this book will find the broader audience it deserves—a general public already feeling the effects of divestiture, a public still puzzled as to why (and how) Bell was dismembered, a public keenly interested in the human dimensions of this unique corporate happening.

I believe this is an important story. Beyond question, it will be a significant contribution to what ultimately will be a rich literature on the break-up of the Bell System. More immediately, it will answer many lingering questions about the events leading to the divestiture decision and the ways in which this monumental task was carried out.

Richard Tanner Pascale
Coauthor of The Art of Japanese Management *and*
Professor of Business Administration
Stanford Graduate School of Business
Palo Alto, California

Preface

This is a book about the break-up of the Bell System. While it focuses on how this monumental task was planned and implemented, every attempt has been made to ensure that it is neither a dry historical account nor a recitation of meetings, status reports, and statistical data. Rather, *Disconnecting Parties* attempts to capture the drama of the government's divestiture order, the managerial challenges to AT&T and its responses, and the lessons that managers and students of business might glean from the experience.

Above all, this is a story about human beings, a family of one million employees who in the critical hour turned the extraordinary spirit that had built and sustained the Bell System to the awesome job of dismantling it. There is a powerful irony in such a positive spirit being applied to an act of corporate self-destruction.

Finally, this is an account of how a historic corporate culture, shaped to function by one set of rules, turned to face a future in which not only its business environment but also all of the rules would change.

For whom has this book been written? It is for those who were part of the action—so that they might see more clearly in these pages how their involvement fit into the larger tapestry of events.

It is for the diverse membership of the managerial community—practitioners and consultants, academicians and their students—who wish to understand the myriad forces leading to the decision to divest and the process by which AT&T executed the agreement. In achieving this understanding, they should be able to extract insights and perceptions that may be useful in conducting their own affairs.

Finally, this book is for a broader audience of general readers who have been increasingly (and not always cheerfully) affected by divestiture, whose interests have been piqued by limited accounts in the media, and who are eager to share an insider's view not only of what happened but also of what it all means.

By virtue of having written this work, I recognize perhaps more than most that no one could have described the entire divestiture scene in every detail and nuance; it was too epic, too turbulent, too multidimensional. What I have managed to assemble, then, represents a singular perspective, one derived from the fortunate central staff vantage point I was assigned at AT&T.

Clearly, there is substantial potential for bias and oversight in telling such a story. Thus, this book is—and should be read as—a narrative of events and opinions from one manager's perspective, not as an official AT&T account. As such, all opinions and observations expressed, unless otherwise noted, are solely the author's.

Acknowledgments

As a reader, I have often been impressed with the degree to which authors have gone out of their way to credit others with assistance and support. Having completed this work, I now understand their gratitude.

People inside and outside the former Bell family have been uniformly generous in filling in bits and pieces of information and helping with my attempt to be as accurate as possible. That I am unable to recognize each does not diminish my appreciation.

I would like, however, to acknowledge the support of Ron Bern and Len Moran and my daughter, Tricia, for editorial assistance. Without their efforts, this book would be considerably less readable.

And to my wife and daughters I will be forever grateful for their understanding, in light of the interminable hours I have had to spend apart from them, laboring in the divestiture vineyards.

W. Brooke Tunstall
Summit, New Jersey
September 15, 1984

Chapter 1

The Historical Context: AT&T Under Siege

Hindsight is always 20/20. In 1984, as the divestiture announcement of that "fateful Friday" in January 1982 receded into the past, it was gradually possible to see the events leading to it as comprehensible, if not predictable.

When the announcement was made, of course, its effect upon all but a few people was one of shock and bewilderment. As Adlai Stevenson once wrote, "Man is the only animal who cannot read the handwriting on the wall until his back is up against it."

The historical handwriting on the Bell System's wall comprised complicated graffiti indeed. As AT&T began its new life in the post-divestiture incarnation, it became possible to examine the record of events that led to the Bell System's demise—to read, translate, and ponder that record in order to approach the future with a sure grasp of the lessons of the past.

Comprehensive historical analysis is not within the scope of a book devoted to AT&T's management of the divestiture process. Divestiture cannot be addressed, however, without some understanding of the complex combination of environmental forces brought to bear on the company in the years preceding. In essence, it is a story of the world's largest company under siege, a chronicle of increasingly successful attempts to limit the Bell System's market presence and constrain its mission. Equally important, it is an account of wrenching ideological conflict between the deepest beliefs of a tradition-proud senior management and the very different priorities of policymakers in the federal government.

A UNIQUE HERITAGE

For the better part of a century the Bell System occupied what must be termed a unique position in American corporate life. Almost from its inception it was identified with an uncommon mission and pursued that mission with exceptional integrity.

The Bell System's unique position, simply stated, was that of a private enterprise with a public trust. The company was responsible to a vast body of shareholders. At the same time, it was responsible for certain interests of the nation as a whole. Seldom, if ever, has an enterprise operated in the public and private spheres with such resounding success in both.

What made this position possible was the astute foresight of those building the telephone system in the early years of this century: regulation would serve as a substitute for competition. It was recognized that the peculiar value of a telecommunications system lay in its universal interconnectivity—a quality achieved far better through coordinated, integrated system building than through the play of competing interests. An alternative had to be found, however, for the financial discipline imposed by the rigors of the market. That alternative would be regulation.

Upon this premise, relationships were forged over the years between the company and its regulators that recognized AT&T's needs as a private enterprise and promoted a set of mutually agreed upon public policy goals. The Communications Act of 1934 formalized industry objectives and established the Federal Communications Commission (FCC) to protect them.

What were those objectives? No one has stated them better than Bell System leaders through the years. In the AT&T Annual Report of 1910, Theodore Vail, revered as the company's founding father, first defined its basic credo this way:

> The telephone system should be universal, interdependent and inter-communicating, affording opportunity for any subscriber of any

exchange to communicate with any other subscriber of any other exchange . . . that some sort of connection with the telephone system should be within reach of all . . . that all this can be accomplished . . . under such control and regulation as will afford the public much better service at less cost than any competition or governmental-owned monopoly.

From Vail's day on, the goals he articulated were the touchstone of all Bell System policies, the motivating vision of all its leaders, the common understanding that linked its employees in their dedication to the famous "spirit of service"—a phrase deriving from an early and exemplary episode in the System's history that fixed the service standard permanently in the corporate culture. Over 60 years later, in a Corporate Policy Seminar in 1975, Chairman John deButts could affirm essentially the same ideals proposed by Vail:

> The Bell System's goal, as I see it, is to ensure "the widest availability of high-quality communications services at the lowest cost to the entire public." That is my definition of the basic social purpose for which this business exists. It is my definition of the public interest.

Noteworthy is deButts's very choice of terms: there are few companies in whose mission statements "social purpose" and "public interest" would be mentioned, much less elevated to the level of central intent. Yet such terms characterized the thinking and indeed the actions of the Bell System throughout its long history.

For those who built the Bell System, the concept of public interest involved above all the twin goals of *universal availability* and *superior quality*. In the service of those goals and of their essential corollaries—service reliability, network efficiency, technological excellence, affordable prices—basic regulatory and corporate policies were established over the years.

Two policy areas in particular stand out as perhaps the critical instruments for realizing the goals outlined above. First are those related to pricing. There could be no more powerful tool for ensuring universal service than the structure of Bell System rates, which set prices below costs for basic residential phone service and covered those costs with revenues from higher-priced long-distance and business services. Thus the service costs were averaged and the charges for them apportioned in such a way as to make reliable telephone service available to the greatest possible number of people.

Equally central was the Bell System's principle of "end-to-end service." The ideals of superior quality and efficiency could best be realized if the entire telecommunications system—from customer terminal through local loop, central office switch, and interstate network—was operated and managed as an integrated process, with unitary responsibility for the whole.

The results, although widely known, are worthy of brief reiteration here. They include a communications infrastructure that links virtually every member of a notoriously scattered, transient population; a scientific laboratory from which some of the major inventions and discoveries of the century have emanated; a vertically integrated manufacturing process of prodigious capacity; and a unified network that, for quality and reliability was the envy of the world. By its own standards, the unique government-corporate experiment that was the Bell System must be judged an extraordinary success.

THE BEGINNING OF CHANGE: NEW TECHNOLOGIES

Why, then, did it come to an end? Most accounts agree that transformation in the telecommunications industry was spurred initially by technological progress. Indeed, the seeds of recent turmoil were latent in technological advances that occurred long before changes in the industry began to make themselves evident.

One such series of advances was the 1948 invention of the transistor and the subsequent development of solid-state electronics. Solid-state capabilities led to a revolution in computer design and operation, and thereby to the explosion of the electronics and computer industries. At roughly the same time, nationwide construction of high-capacity microwave radio relays began. This major new transmission technology held vast potential for both the telecommunications and television fields. Finally, during the next decade there was extensive development of satellite systems. Here was yet another powerful alternative technology for telecommunications.

It is a remarkable fact that all three of these breakthroughs were the fruit of Bell Laboratories scientific research. It was at Bell Labs that the transistor was invented, an achievement honored in 1956 with the Nobel Prize. It was Bell Labs that pioneered the development of microwave radio systems. And in 1962 Bell Labs' Telstar was the first active communications satellite to be placed in orbit.

Even more remarkable, however, is the historical irony that those momentous new technologies were eventually enlisted in the campaigns to undermine and finally to dissolve the Bell System. In the words of a prominent Bell commentator, H. M. Boettinger, in *The Telephone Book: Bell, Watson, Vail and American Life* (Riverwood Publishing, Ltd., 1983):

While each is a major event in the history of telecommunications, we can now see that they were also the tools which would be used to dismantle the Bell System itself. Seldom, outside warfare, can there be such examples of spectacular technology being used for the destruction of the institution which produced them.

That this could come to pass was a function of Bell Labs' long-standing legal obligation to make its patents readily available to all comers—as codified in a Consent Decree with the government in 1956, ending an earlier antitrust action. This, too, as will be seen, was an important feature of the Bell System's special, public-interest-oriented covenant with the public sector. Treated by legal charter as a national resource, Bell Labs disseminated its scientific knowledge and technological achievements. Not surprisingly, many companies and industries looked for ways to take commercial advantage of the new expertise.

In the field of electronics, as the line between computer and communications technologies began to blur there was increasing interest in crossing that line on the part of computer-related industries. Competitive challenge began to appear in markets that had traditionally been considered Bell's domain.

Similarly, in the burgeoning microwave radio industry there emerged potential contenders for competitive entry into the arena of specialized long-distance services. This trend was intensified because the market for such services was itself growing rapidly as large corporations became national in scope.

It should be emphasized that, although technological change alone did not determine the future of the industry, it was one of the sponsors of that future. It encouraged rapid growth in the market for long-distance or interexchange services and made possible the improving cost performance in the various forms of communications. To be sure, the new technologies were bound to be destabilizing. With radically new ways of providing and even conceiving of telecommunications, the field could not have remained the same. Shifts in industry structure were inevitable.

But what shifts would occur and how they would be administered was an open question. There was no single, inevitable telecommunications scenario inherent in the very nature of the new discoveries. Technological advance cannot dictate industrial policy. *It can, and does, offer policymakers new alternatives and choices.*

In the mid-1950s the nation's telecommunications policymakers began to confront such choices. At stake was essentially a political question; the new technologies did not necessarily require full competition any more than the old ones had necessarily required monopoly. It had after all been social function, not technological character, that gave the industry its monopoly status in the first place. As Alvin von Auw writes in his recent study of the Bell System, *Heritage & Destiny: Reflections on the Bell System in Transition* (Praeger, 1983):

> Exchange telephone service and interexchange services have an even more basic claim to being natural monopolies than does the supply of water and gas. That claim is based on the interactive character of both services. Every telephone in every exchange must be able to call and be called by every other telephone in that exchange and in every other exchange. They can do that economically only if they share a common switch or system of switches. The cost advantages of servicing interactive terminals through one network rather than through two or more may change with changing technology. Always, though—the cost advantage is there. It is intrinsic. Exchange service and interexchange services are intrinsic natural monopolies.

Telecommunications had been accorded monopoly status, then, because maximum interconnectivity was the goal. As long as that goal prevailed, some version of monopoly status would need to be maintained and new technologies would need to be implemented accordingly. That was the basic decision before the policymakers. Should preservation of the "interactive character" of telephone service continue to be the highest priority? If so, deployment of new technologies should go forward in a monopoly context. Alternatively, should greater opportunities for competitors now become the top priority? Was there any way to reconcile these conflicting priorities between various areas? What might those areas be? The options were numerous. Only one option—stasis—was not available. The genie of technological innovation, and the questions emerging with it, could not be stuffed back in the bottle.

THE REGULATORY ARENA

It was logical enough that questions would first surface in the regulatory arena. The Federal Communications Commission had been created by the 1934 Communications Act for the purpose of regulating telecommunications in the interest of universal service. By the middle of the 1950s its formal mandate had acquired the dual force of national law and legal fiat. Its role was reaffirmed in court when a

Department of Justice antitrust suit against AT&T and Western Electric—the Bell System's manufacturing and supply unit—was settled in 1956. The resulting Consent Decree issuing from that earlier attempt at divestiture permitted the Bell System to remain intact on the condition that it continue to restrict its business to "common carrier communications subject to regulation."

Clearly, then, legal constraints restricted the Bell System from entering other businesses. What was not explicitly clarified, since the disruptive potential of technological change had not been foreseen by either Congress or the courts, was the issue of other firms entering Bell's business. When aggressive firms armed with new technologies began to demand access to the most attractive telecommunications markets, the FCC was left to its own discretion as to how to respond.

An early exercise of that discretion was the 1956 "Hush-a-Phone" case. The FCC, confronted with a claim from a maker of special terminal equipment, ruled that under certain circumstances a non-Bell terminal could be attached to the network. Three years later, in its "Above 890" ruling, private companies were permitted to use available portions of the microwave radio spectrum. With this pair of decisions the FCC paved the way for the entry of competitive firms into, respectively, the terminal market and the market for intercity private line services.

A series of dockets in the ensuing years constituted a steady process of expanding entry into both markets. In the area of terminal equipment, a major step was taken in the 1968 "Carterfone" decision, which allowed all kinds of non-Bell equipment to be attached to the network, provided only that protective connecting arrangements were used. Six years later the protective-connecting-arrangement proviso was withdrawn, and a program was established for FCC registration of non-Bell equipment attached directly to the network.

A similar trend in the area of private line service saw the "Above 890" decision, which dealt only with individual customers constructing private microwave systems, superseded by a 1969 ruling authorizing a carrier, MCI, to construct such systems. A 1970 ruling went further by allowing "specialized common carriers" to use the Bell System's local exchange networks to complete private line services. And the 1972 "Domsat" decision authorized similar services by means of domestic communications satellites.

It must be noted that the FCC's first deregulatory moves were narrow in scope and intent, designed to open special areas of the market to specific classes of competitors. Although their scope steadily widened, docket decisions up through the early 1970s were oriented toward a specialized-market-sector concept of telecommunications deregulation.

In particular, decisions widening the field for intercity competition referred basically to the private line market: their stated goal was to permit other carriers to provide services not available from the telephone company. This intention is borne out in one of the decade's rare competition-restricting FCC decisions, its denial in 1975 of MCI's "Execunet" service because that service constituted a direct substitute for interexchange telephone service.

If the goals were limited, however, the effects were far-reaching indeed. By allowing competitive carriers to connect their private line systems to Bell's local network, the FCC was *in fact* empowering them to duplicate basic interexchange service—even if in theory it opposed such duplication.

The implications of this development cannot be overestimated. The threat it posed was to the viability not only of the Bell System's interexchange service, known as Message Telecommunications Service, or MTS, but ultimately to the entire system of telephone service.

Why? The explanation lies in the unique Bell System social-pricing structure described earlier. A rival carrier service could be offered for charges appreciably lower than MTS rates, since Bell policy held those rates high enough to support low-priced local service. Offering similar services for lower charges, the alternative carriers were bound to draw customers—particularly the lucrative large business accounts—away from the public switched network in increasing numbers. And the loss of those vital revenues would inevitably jeopardize the entire industry rate structure and the public policy goals it served.

Late in the decade the FCC opened docket 78-72, an inquiry addressed directly to the question of competition in long-distance services. It was soon apparent, however, that the inquiry had come too late. Intercity competition was by this time an inarguable fact, and the question of its desirability largely academic. The inquiry therefore focused on the issue of how to accommodate competition now that it had arrived.

Concurrent with docket 78-72, the agency was addressing the competition issue in the other major market deeply affected by technological change: that arena fashionably known as "compunications." In its "Computer Inquiry II" docket, or CI-II, as it was commonly called, opened in 1978, the FCC took up the claims of those seeking full competition in sectors of the telecommunications market, where computer and communications technologies had begun to converge.

CI-II lasted over 2 years and elicited comments from a variety of interested parties. In 1980 the FCC announced its decision, a major landmark in the deregulation process. That decision drew a distinction between two kinds of services—basic and enhanced—which were differentiated by both technological and market characteristics. Basic services would remain under regulation; enhanced services would be fully deregulated. Also deregulated would be all new customer premises equipment, which increasingly involved the application of solid-state electronic technologies. AT&T could participate in the enhanced services and customer premises equipment (CPE) markets only by establishing a fully separated subsidiary, which would be allowed to compete unrestricted in those markets.

If the effects of deregulatory moves in long-distance service had been gradual and subtle, CI-II was obviously a momentous and quite dramatic change, suddenly opening the way for an explosion of new suppliers of new telecommunications products and services. Most dramatic from the telephone company's point of view, of course, was the requirement to operate henceforth in two entirely different modes.

With regard to the traditional policy goals of the industry, the impacts of this change were at least as profound as those of intercity competition. For if enhanced services must evolve entirely apart from the integrated development and management of the network itself, the potential benefits of advanced technology to the system as a whole are severely constrained. In Alvin von Auw's words, CI-II enacted "structural requirements that, while they may foster competition, do so at the cost of partitioning the network in ways that inhibit the fullest development of its potentialities and widest availability of its services."

The regulatory history of recent years is a saga of successive competitive challenges—mobilized by technological change—that elicited a series of incremental deregulatory actions by the FCC. When the procompetitive effects of early decisions went further than it had envisioned, the agency simply redoubled its deregulatory efforts in order to support the new trends. By the end of the 1970s large sectors of the telecommunications market were fully competitive or on the way to becoming so.

AT&T's role in this saga was, in the words of Board Chairman

Brown, "at first restrained and statesmanlike." Gradually, however, the company grew deeply disturbed by the FCC's evident lack of commitment to the virtues of a system nurtured over decades and unparalleled in quality and kind. Instead of protecting those virtues, FCC rulings were enabling a host of competitors to mount an increasingly effective siege against them.

Bell System top management realized that the company must turn elsewhere for the public validation and reaffirmation it needed to continue to fulfill its mission. Such reaffirmation, to be enduring, could come from only one forum: the Congress of the United States.

THE LEGISLATIVE ARENA

In 1976, at the urging of AT&T and the independent telephone companies, Congress focused its attention on national telecommunications policy. It had not addressed those issues for over 40 years.

In that year both the House and the Senate introduced bills known collectively as the Consumer Communications Reform Act, and, less grandly, as the "Bell Bill." It was true that the legislation had Bell System support. But more was at stake than a display of industrial power: at the heart of the CCRA was a statement of national priorities. "Congress hereby affirms its policy that the integrated interstate telecommunications network shall be structured so as to assure widely available, high quality telecommunications services to all the Nation's telecommunications users." That statement reiterated and reinforced the ideal of universal service that the Congress itself had originally asked the Bell System to serve: The CCRA was not passed. Instead of bringing uncertainty in the industry to an end, as telephone executives had hoped, the act turned out to be merely the opening round of a 6-year legislative battle over telecommunications policy.

Although it was the regulated telephone industry that first took the issue to the legislative arena, its aspiring rivals did not hesitate to follow. They brought their arguments for unfettered competition to the members of Congress with the same political aggressiveness they had displayed in approaching regulators. During the ensuing continuous and often acrimonious debate over the structure and policy of the industry more than a dozen bills were introduced and several hundred people testified before scores of congressional committee meetings.

In 1978 a bill brought before the House, known as the Van Deerlin bill, for its chief sponsor, constituted a thoroughgoing rewrite of the earlier CCRA from a more procompetitive standpoint. New House and Senate legislation in 1979 continued that trend, though it lacked the momentum to come to the floor.

In 1981 yet another round of legislation was mobilized by the FCC's Computer Inquiry II ruling. In the Senate, S. 898 went to the floor and was passed by a startling 90-4 vote. The thrust of that bill was far closer to the philosophy behind the FCC's CI-II than to the tenets of the 1934 act or even those of CCRA a mere 5 years before. More drastic still in its zeal to restructure the industry was the House bill, H.R. 5158, introduced the same year by Congressman Timothy Wirth.

Ironically, then, the legislative attention originally sought to reaffirm the goal of universal service in the face of the FCC's deregulatory broadside ended in a series of legislative proposals affirming the FCC instead. By the time the Senate passed S. 898 it was clear to the Bell System that policymakers' commitment to the country's unified and integrated telecommunications system was rapidly on the wane.

The fight to preserve that commitment was an increasingly uphill battle, in both the regulatory and legislative arenas. It was a fight, moreover, that demanded great political finesse and restraint, in view of the gathering storm in yet a third arena. In the federal court of Judge Harold Greene, a 6-year-old antitrust suit against the Bell System was coming to a head.

THE JUDICIAL ARENA

Since the early 1970s, the route of judicial contest had offered Bell challengers an attractive alternative to regulatory petition or legislative crusade. The 1974 MCI suit against AT&T, charging a variety of antitrust law violations, was only the most prominent of the antitrust suits filed by private companies. With scores of lawsuits in various stages underway throughout the decade, the Bell System was quite literally under siege by litigation.

Looming above the private cases was the suit filed by the U.S. Department of Justice in 1974. The Bell System was charged with monopolizing communications markets, attempting to restrict and eliminate competition from other common carriers, private systems, and manufacturers, and unlawfully favoring Western Electric products. The remedy sought by the Justice Department was total divestiture—the breakup of the Bell System.

AT&T's response was that the case, and indeed antitrust prose-
cutions of the company in general, were inappropriate and unmer-
ited, since the Bell System was constituted to abide by a set of regulatory statutes fundamentally incompatible with antitrust law. As a
regulated monopoly, the Bell System was not only permitted but
obligated to engage in precisely the behaviors antitrust law was
designed to constrain.

At issue was an ideological ambivalence built into the laws of the
land. The basis of antitrust theory is the assumption that monopoly
is intolerable; regulatory theory calls for a common carrier to operate
as a monopoly, with public oversight. Noting this "fundamental
repugnancy," as the lawyers called it, between antitrust and regulatory premises, AT&T argued that the Department of Justice suit
placed the company in an impossible double bind. *It objected to
being punished by antitrust litigation for complying faithfully with
its regulatory charter.*

AT&T was not alone in its objections. Similar positions were
taken by *The Wall Street Journal* in a 1980 editorial statement that
the case "should never have been brought in the first place" and by
The New York Times, which deplored leaving "the fate of the entire
communications industry to a federal judge applying a vague 90-year-
old antitrust law to a single case." In 1981, *Business Week* reported
that "opposition to the nation's 90-year-old antitrust policies is
beginning to sweep the country, and is coming not from corporate
executives but from many economists—including some leading lib-
erals—who say these policies are not serving the economy well."

Appropriate or not, the antitrust charge against Bell was not new.
A similar Justice Department suit, filed in 1949, had been settled with
a Consent Decree in 1956 stipulating the strict regulatory constraints
by which the Bell System must abide—a settlement that left
unsolved, however, the fundamental contradiction embodied in the
laws. Throughout the 1970s, the company's repeated petitions for
appellate courts—up to and including the Supreme Court—to clarify
and resolve those contradictions were not granted.

And so the lawsuits, public and private, went forward. In 1979,
MCI won its 6-year case against the Bell System with a $600 million
award (tripled according to antitrust law to a staggering $1.8 bil-
lion)—that was, however, later reversed.

Two years before, in fact, MCI's competitive crusade had already
gained critical judicial support. Chafing under the FCC's prohibition
of its Execunet service (denied on the ground that it duplicated MTS
service), MCI had taken the issue to court. In 1978, U.S. Court of

Appeals Judge Skelly Wright ruled in MCI's favor. Though given little public attention, Judge Wright's decision was a crucial step in the steady erosion of the Bell System's public mandate. By overturning the FCC's sole order in recent history that protected the System—and supporting, in turn, the tendency to permit competition from those MTS-like services so damaging to the company's rate structure—the court of appeals action was a powerful spur to the gathering momentum of deregulation.

Meanwhile, the government suit proceeded toward trial. Six years and hundreds of millions of dollars were spent as the opposing parties prepared their cases, marshaling thousands of pages of documentary evidence and testimony in what became the most massive civil suit in the nation's history. Pretrial activity accelerated in 1978 when the case was transferred to the energetic jurisdiction of Judge Harold Greene.

At the Justice Department, the cause of Bell System dissolution found a new and ardent champion in Assistant Attorney General William Baxter, whose famous vow to "litigate this case to the eyeballs" dashed hopes that the suit might end, as in the past, with negotiated compromise. AT&T lawyers exploring the possibilities for such compromise were so frustrated by the prosecution's constantly shifting, ever more stringent terms that phases of attempted negotiation came to be dubbed "Quagmires 1, 2, and 3."

United States v. AT&T came to trial in March 1981. For 61 days the Department of Justice presented its case—unfazed in its prosecutory zeal by the fact that other departments of the government objected strongly to the suit. The Commerce Department, for example, had serious reservations about the wisdom of dismembering one of the country's strongest players in the international industrial arena. Even more critical was the position taken by the Department of Defense. The federal government, then, was dramatically divided within itself. But the administration could not intervene. And so the trial continued in high gear as 1981 drew to a close. Even then, few in or outside the company could have predicted the radical nature of the conclusion about to be reached.

AT&T'S BALANCING ACT

The chapters to come will focus on how the largest corporation in the world completed the formidable assignment of managing its own divestiture. No less formidable—and perhaps even more intractable—was the decade-long task of deciding how to respond to the mounting competitive challenges described above.

The record of the Bell System's last, embattled decade is the record of a delicate and complicated balancing act. As a publicly regulated institution entrusted with a charter of public interest goals, its dedication to those goals was felt keenly by every company executive. But as a privately accountable enterprise it was compelled to undertake whatever business changes were necessary to remain prosperous. Throughout the 1970s, therefore, AT&T was busy alerting policymakers to the potential destructiveness of competition while simultaneously changing its internal structure and procedures in order to become more competitive.

With competitors homing in on the most lucrative parts of its market, the company was confronted with the necessity of playing by a new set of rules—those of the competitive marketplace—even as the old rules restricting its own scope of activity remained in place.

A series of internal structural changes were therefore undertaken. In 1978 a massive reorganization realigned the Bell System according to a market sector orientation. Both AT&T and the operating companies were thus mobilized to respond quickly to challenges in various markets. For the first time in Bell history, its many activities began to be seen as discrete market ventures rather than various aspects of a single endeavor. That change was reinforced and expanded in 1980, when the FCC's CI-II decision required AT&T to establish a separate subsidiary for certain markets.

Along with structural adjustments to a changing environment went a major effort to enhance corporate planning capacities. The need for sensitive, flexible planning instruments had not been acute in times of industrial stability; now, however, such instruments were vital to survival. In the early 1970s AT&T instituted a management sciences division to study and articulate the unfamiliar issues and obstacles confronting the management of the business. In the following years a strategic planning organization was formed and this strategic capability was eventually consolidated with financial planning processes.

Through strategic and structural adaptations, then, AT&T was able to assure its shareholders of continuing financial vitality in the face of increasing competition. In the end, of course, the company's new strategic tools simply sharpened its ability to recognize the gravity of its situation. The environmental signposts all pointed one way—and it was not the Bell System's way. In the final months of

1981 it became more and more apparent that something more drastic than internal adjustment was on the horizon.

THE DECISION TO DIVEST

As 1981 drew to a close, the dilemma confronting AT&T executives was twofold. First was the devastating potential consequence of losing the antitrust suit. Second, and equally important in the long run, was the considerable actual harm incurred by the company with every day the trial continued. As to the first consideration, company officials' concern had reached a peak. It had become patently obvious that Judge Greene was biased in favor of the prosecution. In an opinion explaining his refusal of AT&T's request to dismiss the case, printed in the September Federal Supplement, the judge wrote:

> The motion to dismiss is denied. The testimony and the documentary evidence adduced by the government demonstrate that the Bell System has violated the antitrust laws in a number of ways over a lengthy period of time. On the three principal factual issues . . . the evidence sustains the government's basic contentions, and the burden is on defendants to refute the actual showings made in the government's case.

What of AT&T's contention that antitrust standards of behavior were at odds with its historic regulatory mandate? The judge was equally clear:

> By the mid-1970's the FCC had clearly begun to promote competition in telecommunications . . . AT&T had an obligation to follow the more recent FCC policy rather than the Commission's previous policies which may have suited it better.

Never mind that the "previous policies which may have suited it better" had also been the law of the land for half a century; for the judge, the antitrust claim had primary legitimacy. The opinion was in effect a verdict of guilty before the trial was over. Although AT&T was as secure as ever on the essential merit of its case, Judge Greene's statements indicated that unless some kind of settlement was reached the company could expect the worst.

In an interview early in 1983 published in the *Bell Telephone Magazine*, Charles L. Brown, chairman of the board, explicitly described the nature of "the worst." "We faced the prospect of an even more disastrous divestiture—being gutted—by having Western Electric and Bell Labs cut out of the System. We would have lost control of our own technology. And ultimately, I suspect that it would have led to divesting the operating companies anyway." He also said that the Bell System "continued to be confronted with two sets of ground rules: one providing virtually unrestricted entry for our competitors, the other placing severe restrictions on our ability to compete back. Rather than true competition, we faced the worst of all worlds—regulated, contrived competition."

AT&T was the victim of a public policy-making process so chaotic as to allow a government agency single-handedly to usher in a competitive regime while monopoly constraints remained law. The restrictions upon the Bell System had become, in the chairman's words, "a fence with a one-way hole in it."

An immobilized Congress, meanwhile, offered no way out of the crisis. After a full 5 years of agitated debate and legislative drift, which had begun with an effort to protect public interest standards from the erosions of recent FCC policy, it had arrived at legislative proposals that virtually eliminated those standards. And now that the industry was threatened not only with erosion but with dismemberment, the lawmakers were able to provide no clarification or renewal of policy. As Chairman Brown saw it in an address to the Telephone Pioneers of America,

> We are caught on the horns of a dilemma that, were it not so serious, would be ludicrous. On the one hand, some people say that not until the antitrust case has been decided should Congress enact telecommunications legislation. That could be years hence. On the other hand, the Administration says that not until enactment of legislation will it withdraw the antitrust suit. I submit that it is intolerable that an urgently needed national decision should be paralyzed by an Alphonse and Gaston argument over who should go first. It is time . . . for somebody to act.

In December 1981, AT&T acted. Negotiations with the Justice Department were resumed. On January 8, 1982, AT&T and the Justice Department announced to the public their agreement to settle the case.

The agreement was officially known as the Modification of Final Judgment (or MFJ) in that it vacated and replaced the Final Judgment or Consent Decree of 1956 that ended the antitrust suit filed by the government in 1949. The Modification of Final Judgment was, in effect, a new Consent Decree, and it called for AT&T to divest the local portions of its twenty-two Bell operating companies, thereby separating local exchange operations from the other parts of the business. AT&T would continue to carry on the business of intercity service (including intrastate toll service) and terminal equipment (a provision later changed to allow the divested companies into that business as well); it would retain Western Electric and Bell Laboratories. In turn, the government would dismiss the suit and would remove the 1956 Consent Decree restrictions limiting AT&T to provision of common carrier services.

On AT&T's part, action came swiftly once the decision to accept divestiture had been made. Arriving at that decision, on the other hand, had required long and difficult months of analyzing signals and weighing alternatives. Those in the business of hindsight will no doubt be reflecting for years to come on questions of What if...? and Suppose...?

Whatever they conclude, however, some basic assumptions on the company's part cannot be contested. One was that if the trial had run its course, AT&T would likely either have lost everything or become involved in an appeal process lasting for years. Another was that even if the Justice Department challenge had eventually been defeated, the company's corporate structure inevitably made it vulnerable to future antitrust attacks. AT&T executives could foresee that the antitrust threat would hang over the business for as long as it remained "One System".

Finally, it was clear that time was not on the Bell System's side. The longer its traditional markets were eroded and its potential new ones off-limits, the greater the threat to the financial vitality and prosperity of all of its parts.

In the face of these facts, AT&T's decision was based on a lesser of evils choice. Painful though it was, it had the advantage of resolving at one decisive stroke the paralyzing uncertainty that beset the Bell System and defusing the antitrust issue once and for all. It preserved the crucial integration of AT&T's research and manufacturing arms. It gained the company the freedom to use its technology and resources to the fullest in the highly competitive marketplace of the future.

There was one other factor behind the decision to divest—one not frequently mentioned but perhaps, to the executives who made the decision, most important of all. For those executives, a fundamental legacy of Bell System history was its consistent goal of complying with the desires of the public.

Ironically, it was only by breaking with the tradition of an integrated company that the tradition of serving public policy could be faithfully observed. For it was clear that the direction of public policy had undergone a radical change. While the ideal of universal service was still professed, the means of sustaining it was replaced by competitive supply.

For the Bell System, then, a tradition of serving the public led finally to an agreement upon divestiture. Reflecting upon the political environment of the times, Chairman Brown commented that "the fundamental reality was the widely held public and governmental perception that the Bell System is simply too big and too powerful." Then, recalling that the economist Maynard Keynes had once referred to Woodrow Wilson as a "blind Don Quixote," the chairman, in a 1980 issue of the *Bell Telephone Magazine*, went on to articulate his own perspective on the Bell System's momentous decision:

> I would not want this business—or me—to be accused of being a "blind Don Quixote," unable to assimilate what's happening outside merely because of an *a priori* belief that the Bell System has to stay in one piece.

Chapter 2

Divestiture Planning Diary

Like a great revolution, divestiture can be viewed from many perspectives, each providing its own rich accounting of the events and personalities that gave it shape and character.

Each of these perspectives—for example, the legal issues involved, the financial developments, the legislative matters—presents its own special saga; each contributes its own critical dimensions. Yet to encompass the larger story, the reader may require a wider overview than any discipline-specific sequence of events might supply. This "diary," then, will reveal the broad management process that constituted the planning and implementation of divestiture through the eight quarters of 1982 and 1983. It will describe how the project unfolded; how divestor and divestees joined forces to forge hundreds of decisions, only a few of which had to be submitted to higher authority; and how the intensity of effort of thousands of employees met a challenge of monumental proportions.

In this connection it should be declared for the record that in rallying to their last great task, Bell System people committed themselves despite their own distaste for its conclusion. In the words (only slightly bowdlerized) of one participant: "The most amazing thing was that so many people really busted their backsides doing something that they really didn't believe was a good idea."

FIRST QUARTER, 1982: THE LONG ROAD AHEAD

On January 9, 1982, the conservative *The New York Times* carried a banner eight-column headline on page 1 in type reserved for wars and other national calamities: "AT&T Split Up, Transforming Industry." Hours later, the first editions of the somewhat more colorful *New York Post* hit the streets with this perhaps prophetic headline: "Ma Bell Gets a Divorce; We'll Pay The Alimony."

Throughout the nation, the news called out to all within reach of newspaper, radio, or television. The great media derby had begun: a tireless scramble for new angles for the next edition's page 1, the next magazine issue's cover story, the lead item on the six o'clock news.

Inside the Bell System, the hours that followed the announcement were characterized by profound shock, disbelief, and often anger, soon to be followed by a rush of unanswered questions. The foremost of these were, how might the awesome task ordained by the Justice Department and formalized by Judge Greene's Modification of Final Judgment ever be accomplished, and, more immediately, where might such a task even begin?

As staff units gathered to pore over the document, they were surprised to discover that it comprised merely 14 double-spaced pages of general principles and that it constituted the only guidelines for their unprecedented task. Nonetheless, they promptly began the effort to interpret its intent and requirements as they sought to sketch broad outlines of "get started" plans.

One Bell Operating Company (BOC) president, hoping to get some grip on the project, asked his staff to develop questions that would have to be answered before the terms of the decree could be executed. The response was a 2-inch-thick binder with thousands of them, organized by departments. Similarly, at AT&T, Chief Planning Officer John Segall asked his staff to prepare a list of issues derived from the MFJ and a general approach to the project. In such fashion the management of divestiture was set in motion, with the identification of questions that needed answers and issues that needed resolution.

These initial substantive efforts began on Saturday, January 9, the first of 100 consecutive weekends during which thousands of Bell System people, working singly and in groups, would labor on details of planning and implementation —recalling that old American proverb: "Hats off to the past, coats off to the future."

Beginning Steps

AT&T's Office of the Chairman (its top five officers) met with other key executives on Monday, January 11, in a day-long session. The meeting began with a review of reactions to the settlement by the corporation's various constituencies. Next, the possible legal, regulatory, and legislative implications were discussed in considerable detail. Finally, the planning and implementation of divestiture were addressed. In this context it was immediately evident not only that the project would have to be managed apart from the day-to-day conduct of the business, but that it would have to be planned in new and unaccustomed fashion, since normal processes were inadequate for an effort of such dimensions. If a guiding philosophy were needed, it might have been fashioned from Abraham Lincoln's remarks to Congress 100 years earlier: "The dogmas of the quiet past are inadequate to the stormy present. . . . As our case is new, so we must think anew and act anew. We must disenthrall ourselves."

Together, the members of the Office of the Chairman began their active management of divestiture by outlining six major questions that would require answering in order to move forward in compliance with the MFJ:

1. What should the structural form of the divested companies be, operationally and financially?

2. Would prior studies of interexchange/intraexchange divisions suffice in carrying out the terms of the decree?

3. How would the access charge structure be determined? That is, what rate formula would be used to replace the former subsidies for local service?

4. What market access issues were in store for Western Electric?

5. How could the corporation insure that employee and shareholder interests were adequately represented?

6. What organizational framework was required for planning and implementing the Modification of Final Judgment?

In retrospect, it was a felicitous formulation of the issues. In fact, the effort to resolve the questions in just these six areas would continue to supply the major thrusts driving the divestiture project for the next 2 years. To be sure, the officers' foresight was not entirely providential. Six years' involvement in the antitrust case, including preparation of testimony for scores of witnesses, had provided a solid grounding in the issues. Further, for more than 2 years special teams of staff experts at AT&T had been studying the financial and operational implications of proposed congressional legislation. And while none of these exercises simulated divestiture directly, some useful hypotheses had been considered: for example, redistricting exchange boundaries, access charge mechanisms, regionalization, and so on.

Clearly, AT&T Chairman Brown's much-quoted remark, "It wasn't our idea," referred, then, to the repugnant nature of the decision rather than to any lack of forethought on contigencies. The six major questions had been gleaned from considerable prior reflection. Beyond doubt, there would be surprises, difficulties, prolonged uncertainties. But this codification of the major avenues of pursuit served to provide the framework for beginning.

Organizational Framework and Management Philosophy

The sixth question, pertaining to organizational framework and managerial philosophy, took on special significance from the very outset. The task of executing divestiture was such that normal modes of project management—say, those for a moon landing or transcontinental pipeline—would simply not suffice. Tight central control of all facets of the project could not succeed because there was too much uncertainty, too much interdependent complexity. (To Bell managers it was "like cloning a 747 seven times over in midflight," or "more like pulling taffy apart than breaking a cookie eight ways.")

AT&T's principal officers therefore set in place a managerial apparatus designed more to facilitate than to direct. General principles would be framed by joint high-level AT&T-Bell Operating Company task groups. Then, second-layer AT&T-BOC task groups would develop plans and guidelines from these principles. Finally, accountable line organizations, working with these plans and guidelines, would carry out the details of implementation.

This strategy had many virtues, not least among them that it would provide enough freedom for "subject-matter experts"— employees with special knowledge of operational or administrative details—to innovate and solve rather than wait for answers from on high. Moreover, it would provide for participative AT&T-BOC direction, as well as for easy access to decision makers on critical issues.

This participative mode had been a style of management familiar to Bell managers for decades. It served them especially well in this critical hour. They knew that any attempt to manage divestiture by providing a priori answers from an all-knowing central Zeus would be doomed to failure. And there was simply no place in the tight divestiture time frame for failure—or even for false starts.

Ironically, this participatory mode stood in stark contrast to assertions and anxieties expressed outside the Bell System. Analysts and writers gravely assured newspaper readers that AT&T management held all the cards and would almost certainly deal them in favor of the surviving AT&T, at the clear expense of the BOCs. And yet at every meeting attended by this writer—and they were many—the critical element in decision making was always manifest: to balance the interests of shareholders, customers, employees, and the public at large. It was, in fact, the readily accepted traditional standard of the Bell System.

This is not to say that there were not many bitterly debated issues among the factions; indeed there were. There is, for example, the remark reportedly made by a bruised participant elsewhere: "This was no Bell System love-in." It *is* to say, however, that the management process for divestiture was one in which the interests of the constituencies were paramount.

Presidential Study Groups

The first meeting of AT&T officers and Bell Operating Company presidents, after the Washington press conference, was held on January 21, the ninth working day after the announcement. A small card was at each participant's position at the table. It was placed at the initiative of Chairman Brown, to set the tone, and read as follows:

> If there is any period one would desire to be born in, is it not
> the age of revolution; when the old and the new stand side by

side and admit to being compared; when the energies of all men are searched by fear and hope; when the historical glories of the old can be compensated by the rich possibilities of the new era? This time, like all times, is a very good one, if we but know what to do with it.

RALPH WALDO EMERSON
Five Bells in The Night

The message was clear. How divestiture would be achieved would depend on what the participants in this room—together, disenthralled—would do with it. Moving from philosophy to action, the chairman announced the formation of six presidents' study groups, each to consist of four or five BOC presidents, to address the central issues, thus assuring ample operating company representation from the start.

Each company president was asked to indicate the issues, and hence the study group, he preferred to work with. The issues, and the groups formed to address them, are shown in Table 1. The array presented there by no means encompassed the full range of planning. Operational matters, contracts, trademark and trade name use, the apportionment of information systems, and the handling of billing services are but a few of the manifold activities conducted by other staff units throughout the corporation. But the study groups did serve the key function of establishing, as it were, the constitutional principles on major issues that would guide the planners down the line in making decisions.

Table 1   Divestiture: Presidents' Study Groups

Critical issue	AT&T chairman	Operating company presidents
Corporate structure	W. S. Cashel	W. R. Bunn South Central Bell Telephone Company W. L. Weiss Illinois Bell Telephone Company J. A. MacAllister Northwestern Bell Telephone Company

Table 1 Divestiture: Presidents' Study Groups (*continued*)

Critical issue	AT&T chairman	Operating company presidents

		A. V. Smith
		    Pacific Northwest Bell
		        Telephone Company

Asset assignment	W. S. Cashel	W. L. Mobraaten
		    The Bell Telephone
		        Company of Pennyslvania/
		    The Diamond State
		        Telephone Company
		W. R. Bunn
		    South Central Bell
		        Telephone Company
		W. L. Weiss
		    Illinois Bell Telephone
		        Company
		R. W. Kleinert
		    AT&T Company Long Lines
		        Department

Drawing exchange boundaries	K. J. Whalen	R. J. Marano
		    New Jersey Bell Telephone
		        Company
		R. T. Dugan
		    Cincinnati Bell Inc.
		D. C. Staley
		    New York Telephone
		        Company
		R. K. Timothy
		    The Mountain States
		        Telephone and Telegraph
		        Company

Personnel considerations	K. J. Whalen	W. C. Mercer
		    New England Telephone and
		        Telegraph Company
		R. E. Allen
		    The Chesapeake and
		        Potomac Telephone
		        Companies
		W. E. MacDonald
		    The Ohio Bell Telephone
		        Company
		D. E. Easlick
		    Michigan Bell Telephone
		        Company

Table 1 Divestiture: Presidents' Study Groups (*continued*)

Critical issue	AT&T chairman	Operating company presidents

Centralized staff	T. E. Bolger	A. W. VanSinderen
		  Southern New England
		    Telephone Company
		D. E. Guinn (Chmn.)
		  The Pacific Telephone and
		    Telegraph Company/Bell
		    Telephone Company of
		    Nevada
		R. E. Allen
		  The Chesapeake and
		    Potomac Telephone
		    Companies
		P. A. Campbell
		  Indiana Bell Telephone
		    Company, Incorporated
		Z. E. Barnes
		  Southwestern Bell
		    Telephone Company

Access charges	K. J. Whalen	W. L. Mobraaten
		  The Bell Telephone
		    Company of Pennsylvania/
		    The Diamond State
		    Telephone Company
		D. C. Staley
		  New York Telephone
		    Company
		R. J. Marano
		  New Jersey Bell Telephone
		    Company
		J. L. Clendenin
		  Southern Bell Telephone and
		    Telegraph Company
		T. J. Saenger (Pres.)
		  The Pacific Telephone and
		    Telegraph Company/Bell
		    Telephone Company of
		    Nevada

Early Turmoil: A Shingle Factory in a Hurricane

Where the immense job of planning divestiture actually came to rest, however, was squarely on the shoulders of the AT&T headquarters staff units, known as the "general departments." At 15,000 strong, in 1982, it was easily the largest headquarters group in American industry. For decades this organization had had for its charter the integration and seamless cohesion of the Bell System's many parts, in conjunction with operating company staffs. Now it was to turn its formidable skills and knowledge to precisely the opposite mission.

Since, as noted, no comparable antecedent existed for divestiture, no profound vision for its management could be summoned. The MFJ provided merely the requirements in broad legal terms, and only a few highly specialized staff members had been involved in deliberations prior to the signing of the decree.

However, because complexity was in effect their study, headquarters people could discern at least the outlines of the undertaking. They knew the storyboard was something like this: new, divested companies, each with anywhere from $15 to $23 billion in assets, would have to be launched, if not ex nihilo, then certainly with a markedly altered character; 70 million customer accounts, comprising 200 million customer records, would have to be split and allotted among new segments of AT&T and the relevant regional Bell operating companies; 24,000 buildings and 177,000 motor vehicles would have to be reassigned; new sales and service offices would have to be established, staffed, and set in operation across the country; 136,000 employees would have to be transferred across company borders within the Bell System; hundreds of new tariffs would have to be filed with regulatory commissions; scores of computerized operational support systems would have to be torn apart, redesigned, reprogrammed, tested, and debugged; and the remaining AT&T would have to undergo radical reorganization.

Perhaps the most trying aspect of these tasks was their interdependence. For example, access charges were dependent on asset division. Asset division was dependent on how "exchange boundaries" (that is, the boundaries of calling areas to be served by the divested companies) were drawn. Approval of exchange boundaries was dependent on joint AT&T-BOC team study and analysis, as well as on approvals from the Justice Department and the court. And so it went. In effect, it was a giant jigsaw puzzle disassembled, the pieces strewn about, with no one knowing with any precision what the final picture was supposed to look like. Or, in the words of one manager, not unlike "a shingle factory in a hurricane."

The Process Begins: Setting Divestiture Assumptions

An initial breakthrough came, as so often happens in difficult times, from an unexpected quarter. Early in February a midlevel staff member named Mike Farmer came to see the need for a comprehensive set of divestiture assumptions. Farmer, temporarily assigned to AT&T's corporate planning division from Indiana Bell, realized that where uncertainty existed—as it did in almost every area—even best-guess assumptions would serve to move the project off dead center. To draw such assumptions effectively, the views of hundreds of experts would have to be tapped. But Farmer had an idea. Acting on his own, he sat down, pencil in hand, and analyzed the MFJ paragraph by paragraph, sentence by sentence, word by word, extracting every potential nuance of intent and meaning. From this analysis, he constructed a list of hundreds of questions, issues, and implications.

The list was then distributed within AT&T to all the departmental subject-matter experts—or SMEs, in the inevitable acronym—in operations, finance, regulatory, human resources, public relations, etc. to comment on, expand, and clarify. Concurrently, the central staffs in the operating companies were encouraged to engage in the same exercise, viewing the MFJ from their own vantage.

Hundreds of comments, answers, and corrections rode the returning tide to Farmer's desk. Combined, they became part of the critical mass out of which Farmer rendered the first rough sketch of the divestiture picture—the initial set of assumptions that would drive the management effort for the next 2 years.

The "assumption set" covered every conceivable subject area: public policy, organizational structure, transfer of personnel, division of assets, billing arrangements, and many more. Even in this first version, the level of detail could be fairly precise, as shown in these randomly selected examples:

> **A208** Facilities and other assets which serve both AT&T and one or more BOCs will be assigned to the BOCs where they are the predominant user.

> **C156** Terminal equipment used for maintenance of interexchange systems will be assigned to AT&T.
>
> **C600** Bell Operating Companies will be permitted under tariff to bill customers for the interexchange services of any requesting qualified carrier.

As it was meant to do, the rough sketch drew fire. Subject-matter experts—even those who had supplied opinions in response to Farmer's original questions—objected to, corrected, and touched up the finer details here and there, in effect sharpening the focus in areas they claimed as their own. The process was working.

In the months to follow, the divestiture assumption set would be continuously revised but would always serve as the core document from which planning could proceed. It would be the baseline for other key documents, including the Planning Guidelines for Bell Operating Companies, the Implementation Guidelines to be released in phases during late 1982 and early 1983, and the Plan of Reorganization that had to be submitted to the Justice Department under the terms of the MFJ.

With the assumption set virtually a script, each department set about defining its particular role in the divestiture preparations. Under Chief Planning Officer John Segall, who would play a pivotal part in the 1982 planning effort, the corporate planning division worked on overall coordination, while the financial management staff began to identify and analyze major corporate concerns. Strategic planners Lee Cutcliff and Larry Hendrickson deployed interdisciplinary teams in a kind of reconnaissance of principal issues to be confronted, and financial analysts Ed Goldstein and Dick Romano began pondering other significant questions pertaining to the breakup: What would be the most appropriate structural arrangement for the divested companies? How can the MFJ's requirement to divest the Bell Operating Companies in "financially viable condition" best be carried out? What arrangement would best serve shareholders, customers, employees, and the nation at large?

As mentioned previously, AT&T planners were already in the throes of another government mandate. This was the FCC's Computer Inquiry II order to form a separate subsidiary by January 1, 1983, to provide, on a detariffed basis, all new customer premises equipment (telephones, switchboards or PBXs, and so on) and "enhanced services" (for example, storage and forwarding of customers' voice messages). The extent of this change alone involved a complete overhaul of AT&T's marketing, sales, and distribution procedures. Since the FCC's mandate was not affected by the settlement of January 8, planning for CI-II had to continue as the corporation dealt with the early chaos of divestiture.

The Process Expands: Communicating with the BOCs

Meanwhile, operating company staffs were somewhat hampered in their own planning until the joint task groups at AT&T, groping for answers to as yet undefined questions, could provide the companies with the necessary guidelines. In consequence, the feelings of apprehension experienced in the companies engendered, perhaps inevitably, a degree of suspicion that AT&T was withholding information. One result of this uneasiness, however, was beneficial. The companies insisted that integrated guidelines, rather than separate, uncoordinated department-by-department segments, be issued. What emerged, accordingly, was a better product. Later, in fact, this early integration would prove a boon.

As the end of the first quarter neared, the management framework had been erected, presidential study groups had been set in place, corporate assumptions had been formulated, schedules had been drawn, and each of the corporate staffs was in pursuit of its respective objective.

As the early confusion began to lift somewhat on the mass of the challenge yet to be scaled, many sought to describe it in precise terms. Interestingly, no corporate analyst or veteran business reporter managed it as well as Michael Novak, a theologian, in a *Bell Telephone Magazine* of 1983: "I am glad not to be presiding over the Bell System's gargantuan change, trying to make sure the many are kept informed, their anxieties lowered, their spirits kept high; and at the same time, seeing to it that service is not only continued but also improved, profits are sustained to guarantee long-term survival, and sound decisions about technology are made." Amen.

SECOND QUARTER, 1982: "INCREDIBLE AND COMPLEX"

The development for the entire Bell System of two major sets of planning guidelines comprised the central planning effort of the second quarter: the first set in compliance with the FCC's CI-II order; the second to execute the terms of the Consent Decree. The responsibility was hardly new to the AT&T staff. In fact, it was its historic role to develop "plans and policies common to all," a mission defined early in the century by Bell's chief corporate architect, Theodore N. Vail. But never before had the circumstances been quite so daunting.

Under normal conditions, such comprehensive documents would have taken up to 2 years to produce. Each, after all, absorbed thousands of hours of work and comprised thousands of pages. Each presented an overall conceptual scheme, an applicable assemblage of assumptions about the course of external events, and a complete compilation of instructions to AT&T's subsidiary units.

But conditions were far from normal; the guidelines had to be eady by the time the court approved the MFJ. Exactly when that would happen no one knew, but Judge Greene was known for his expeditiousness—to say the least. AT&T planners assumed it could come as early as July 1. Thus, instead of a routinely industrious 2 years, AT&T had a scant and fevered 3 months—from the beginning of April to the end of June—to get the job done.

Not surprisingly, a request came down from the Office of the Chairman for a schema of some kind, a diagrammatic projection of the planning process envisioned. Complying, staffers developed two bar charts depicting the major planning activities and the milestone internal and external events anticipated throughout 1982 and 1983 (see Figures 1 and 2). The chairman's reaction, conveyed in a handwritten note, succinctly expressed the sentiments of most parties to the effort: "Incredible and complex. I hope you can keep it untangled."

"You" became the operative word. No master plan would descend. And keeping it untangled would be the job of the AT&T-BOC planners—further encouragement of the loose-knit, jurisdictional sway designed to allow staff-level people maximum authority, and accountability, to plan and execute their own designs.

The Directors Planning Group

To help "untangle" snags in the two interlocking government mandates and produce two coherent, integrated sets of planning guidelines, more than a thousand additional specialists from subsidiary units joined the headquarters staff. At the core of the ensuing process

1982　1983

EXTERNAL

DIVESTITURE 1/1/84

CONSENT DECREE EFFECTIVE 7/1

COURT OF APPEALS ACTION ON CHI APPEAL 7/82

REORGANIZATION PLAN FILING TO DOJ 1/1/83

INTERNAL

PRES CONF. 5/10-5/14 | PLANNING GL TO BOCs 7/1 | DIVESTITURE IMPLEMENTATION GL TO BOCs 9/1 | BOC PLANS TO AT&T 9/1 | PRES CONF. 11/8-11/12 | FSS BEGINS OFFERING NEW CPE 1/1/83 | POTENTIAL FILING OF RATE CASE ON PRO FORMA BASIS 1/1/83 | PRES. CONF. 5/5 | PRES. CONF. 11/-11

Months: APRIL MAY JUNE JULY AUG SEP OCT NOV DEC JAN FEB MAR APRIL MAY JUNE JULY AUG SEP OCT NOV DEC

MAJOR PLANNING ACTIVITIES

CORPORATE

DEVELOPMENT OF PLANNING ASSUMPTIONS FOR BOCs & GENERAL DEPTS. - (TUNSTALL)
COMPLETE 4/16

PRESIDENTIAL STUDY GROUPS (SEGALL)
COMPLETE 5/8

COMMITMENT BUDGET CYCLE - (HARRINGTON) 1983-84 W/BIFURCATION
DATA REQUEST 5/21
PRELIMINARY BUDGET 7/29
BD OF DIRECTORS REVIEW 12/15

1984-87 W/BIFURCATION & DIVESTITURE

BOC PLANNING GUIDELINES (TUNSTALL)
PRE-COMMITMENT VIEW GL TO BOCs 5/21
DATA REQUEST 7/1
PLANNING GUIDELINES TO BOC 7/1
BOC RESPONSE 9/1
BOC PLAN RESPONSE 9/1
DIVESTITURE IMPLEMENTATION GLs TO BOCs 11/1
BEGIN DIVESTITURE DOTTED LINE RESTRUCTURING 1/1/83

IPRAP (LOB PLANNING) (GOLDSTEIN)
ISSUE LOB GL 3/5
PRELIM. LOB PLANS TO CORP MGT 5/14
REV OF PRELIM LOB PLANS BY D/C 5/17-6/18
REVISED LOB PLANS TO CORP MGT 10/1
Q&C LOB REVIEW 10/1-10/20

CONSTRUCTION PLANS (STECKER)
FULL VIEW OF 1982, 83, 84 REQUESTED 7/1
RESPONSE DUE 10/1

GENERAL DEPARTMENTS REALIGNMENT (TUNSTALL)
PLANNING GL TO GEN DEPTS 3/22
GEN DEPTS RESPONSE 5/10
QC APPROVAL 7/1
GRADUAL REALIGNMENT OF GENERAL DEPARTMENTS

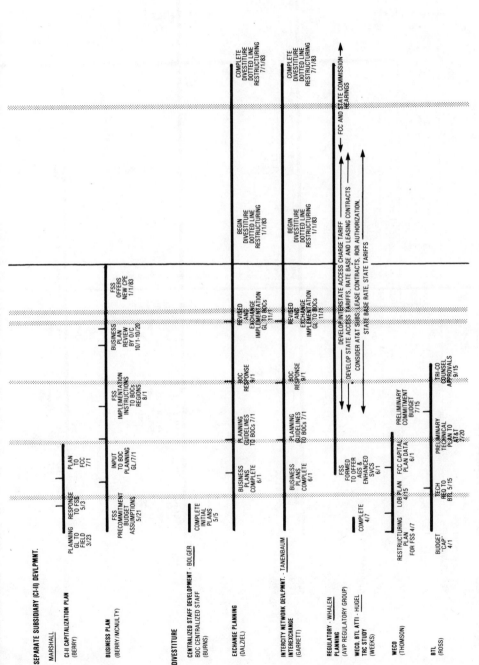

FIGURE 1. CI-II and divestiture planning timelines.

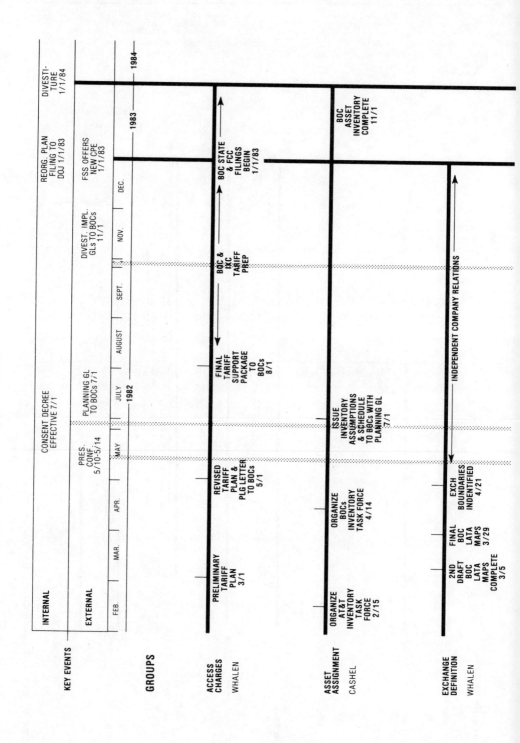

KEY EVENTS

| INTERNAL | | CONSENT DECREE EFFECTIVE 7/1 | | | REORG. PLAN FILING TO DOJ 1/1/83 | | DIVESTI- TURE 1/1/84 |

EXTERNAL: PRES. CONF. 5/10-5/14 · PLANNING GL TO BOCs 7/1 · DIVEST. IMPL. GLs TO BOCs 11/1 · FSS OFFERS NEW CPE 1/1/83

FEB. | MAR. | APR. | MAY | JULY | AUGUST | SEPT. | NOV. | DEC.

1982 — **1983** — **1984**

GROUPS

ACCESS CHARGES
WHALEN

- PRELIMINARY TARIFF PLAN 3/1
- REVISED TARIFF PLAN & PLG LETTER TO BOCs 5/1
- FINAL TARIFF SUPPORT PACKAGE TO BOCs 8/1
- BOC & IXC TARIFF PREP
- BOC STATE & FCC FILINGS BEGIN 1/1/83

ASSET ASSIGNMENT
CASHEL

- ORGANIZE AT&T INVENTORY TASK FORCE 2/15
- ORGANIZE BOCs INVENTORY TASK FORCE 4/14
- ISSUE INVENTORY ASSUMPTIONS & SCHEDULE TO BOCs WITH PLANNING GL 7/1
- BOC ASSET INVENTORY COMPLETE 11/1

EXCHANGE DEFINITION
WHALEN

- 2ND DRAFT BOC LATA MAPS COMPLETE 3/5
- FINAL BOC LATA MAPS 3/29
- EXCH BOUNDARIES INDENTIFIED 4/21
- INDEPENDENT COMPANY RELATIONS

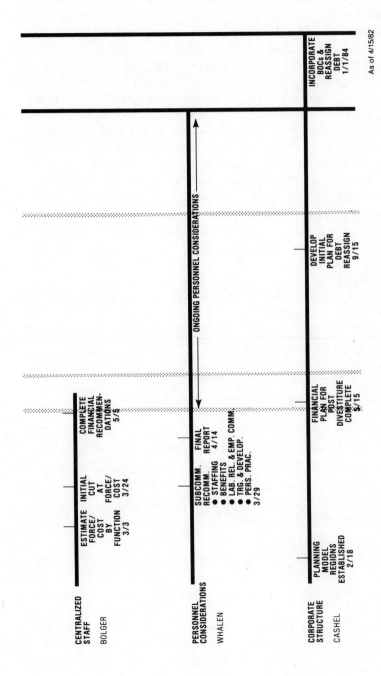

FIGURE 2. Presidents' study groups timelines.

was set a nucleus of corporate planning managers to provide central coordination.

As with Mike Farmer, a crucial boost came from the enterprise and initiative of a single individual. Jim Cullen, a director in corporate planning who had come from New Jersey Bell via the Sloan School of Management, assembled a small group of middle managers in key planning roles and began to hold informal weekly meetings. Soon the gatherings provided a special forum for wide-ranging discussion of divestiture issues, information sharing, and strategic planning. By early April, Cullen's group had been formalized by name and acronym—Directors Planning Group (DPG)—and by regularly scheduled Tuesday meetings (plus some in between), all with pre-planned agendas. In short order, other leading players in the divestiture drama recognized that the DPG's meetings were the place where "cross-cutting" issues could be aired and where the broad outline of divestiture could be given a kind of run-through or showcase. Before long, an SRO crowd of fifty to sixty people was packing the conference room at every one of the group's sessions.

A glance at the minutes of those early meetings confirms the DPG's role as the prime mover in developing the two sets of guidelines and as the permanent focal point for the overall planning of divestiture. Among many entries were the following:

April 6   Corporate Planning will initiate action to assure that the mechanics of producing guidelines will not jeopardize the May 21 and June 1 issue dates.

An outline of the planning process control was distributed.

The treatment of Customer Premise Equipment was cited as an issue Mr. Benedict will discuss on April 8, 1982.

April 8   Members were asked to review CI-II assumptions for inclusion in May 21 Guidelines.

All functional guidelines are due to be complete by May 4.

Clear ground rules are needed for transferring people between new entities.

In matters of general principle, the DPG was guided by the top-level discussions of the six presidential study groups. At the other extreme, DPG members consulted the subject-matter experts on matters of ever-increasing detail. Literally thousands of SMEs, many borrowed from the operating companies, made contributions.

One phenomenon of the DPG meetings might be characterized as mitosis—"cells" of divestiture work splitting off into management structures and lives of their own. The most notable example involved the prodigious task of organizing and controlling the operational aspects of divestiture. Owing to its magnitude and importance, Operations would have to develop its own management apparatus to plan and control the separation and restructuring of the network, business offices, service order systems, and installation and maintenance practices, to name but a few of its functions.

Operations was only the first to initiate a comprehensive effort. Other cells parted to manage such tributary matters as personnel transfers, customer equipment asset assignment, and the redeployment of the 15,000-member AT&T headquarters staff, each undertaking requiring its own separate and sustained effort. All the cells, however, would continue to retain ties to the DPG, somewhat as satellites to the central body.

As the July 1 deadline neared, 7 A.M. meetings, working lunches, midnight calls, and 7-day work weeks became ever more commonplace. The pressure summoned all sorts of hidden resources, including, apparently, a flair for the epigrammatic, as the following appeared on a Basking Ridge bulletin board: "On any project, adrenalin flows in direct proportion to the nearness of the completion date!" On Wednesday, June 30, 1000 five-volume sets of the divestiture planning guidelines were on their way to twenty-two Bell Operating Companies by courier. As issuer, I was asked who had written them. My answer, of course, was that *everyone* had written them.

The accomplishment was all the more impressive in that those working on it had strong, sometimes emotional reservations about the entire project. Many believed deeply that divestiture would not serve the interests of customers, the industry, or the nation as a whole. They recognized that they were compelled by circumstances to accept it; they did not feel required to agree with it. As was noted elsewhere in connection with the preparations for the Washington press conference of January 8, no one on the AT&T side had to be coached or cued to contain enthusiasm for the whole affair.

The same sense of dismay prevailed in the BOCs as they received the guidelines. But, like the AT&T planners, they bowed to the inevitable. In each company, central planners immediately began subdividing the binders and dealing them out to subject-matter experts in each department. There were few surprises within those guidelines, since the extensive forces borrowed from the BOCs had kept the home office abreast of evolving details. What did cause considerable stir was the immensity of the aggregate planning job revealed. Nonetheless, with characteristic energy, the BOCs accepted the planning baton as it was passed to them and began to develop their own specific plans—recognizing all the while, of course, that the guidelines were not the final word, and that many assumptions remained to be tested.

Meanwhile, if only for the moment, the pressure was off the planners at AT&T headquarters. During that all-too-brief respite, it occurred to the writer how unfortunate it was that there was no cartoonist like World War II's Bill Mauldin around to record the combination of hardship and humor that prevailed in the divestiture trenches. Had there been, he might have depicted an office scene, darkness beyond the windows, a clock showing midnight, and a tired, unshaven "Willie" and "Joe," surrounded by a sea of paper, trying to read the fine type of the guidelines through eyes dull with fatigue. The caption might read: "I wonder what Baxter and Greene are doing right now?"

THIRD QUARTER, 1982:
ERECTING THE SUPERSTRUCTURE

As the Bell System awaited Judge Greene's formal endorsement of the MFJ during the summer of 1982, events in another arena were coming to a head. A bill had been introduced in the House of Representatives which, if voted into law, would override the Consent Decree. Sponsored by Representative Timothy Wirth of Colorado, H.R. 5158 was designed to place more restrictions on AT&T than had any legislative proposal in a nearly decade-long attempt to revise national telecommunications policy. The stated purpose of H.R. 5158 was to increase competition in telecommunications. However, in AT&T's view, the bill would have nothing less than a "disastrous impact on employees, shareholders and customers." For the first time in its long history, the company asked its shareholders and employees to express themselves on the matter to their congressional representatives.

The response was gratifying. As *The Washington Post* of April 15,

1982 reported, "The letters come in each day by the boxful—angry, insistent, occasionally heart-rending. By some Senate and House members' reckoning, they constitute the most massive outpouring of mail on a single subject to hit Capitol Hill since the Saturday Night Massacre at the height of the Watergate scandal."

The response was also effective. On July 21, in what *The New York Times* called "a stunning victory for AT&T," the effort to enact H.R.5158 was abandoned. But this rallying round—this "last hurrah"—to defeat the Wirth bill was also a massive demonstration that the dissolution of the Bell System remained repugnant, indeed traumatic, to many. As social scientist Kai Erikson wrote in a 1982 *Bell Telephone Magazine* article,

> How anything so vast, so bureaucratic, so dedicated to efficiency, so tightly organized, can still retain the feeling of a close community is something of a mystery. In part at least, this community feeling must be breathed into the System by the warmth and good will of the employees who have invested so much of themselves in their place of work. But whatever its origin, it is there. Even a casual visitor can see that many are joined by the sense of shared identity, and even kinship, that lies at the heart of true community.

Or, as novelist Alex Haley wrote, "There is not another drama to match it within U.S. industry."

Nonetheless, in the last act of that drama, even the most seriously disaffected worked toward the inescapable climax. People in all parts of AT&T and its subsidiaries came together in interdisciplinary boards, ad hoc committees and task forces to execute the plans and principles developed in the first two quarters. In this fashion, a divestiture management apparatus took shape.

While it is unfeasible to list the hundreds of groups that formed, the representation of the major boards and committees, which appears as Table 2 (page 40), provides at least a sense of the whole apparatus, and hints at its diversity and scope.

As noted, this is an incomplete representation of the divestiture apparatus. It does not include the special teams that supported each group or the counterpart boards and committees formed in each region. Finally, it does not reveal that, whereas planning activity in the first two quarters was confined to a limited core of people, by the third quarter many thousands were enrolled.

The managerial network that evolved had several significant features. One was the spontaneity of its evolution. Although to some degree controlled, it grew faster and more effectively than corporate

Table 2 Major Divestiture Boards and Committees

Committee	Function
Oversight	
Presidential Study Group	Addressing six major areas of divestiture
Restructure Implementation Board	Overall coordination and tracking, issue identification, review, resolution
Operations	
Operations Divestiture Board	Responsibility for overseeing disaggregation of operations functions
Business Office Divestiture Project (BODP)	Developing business office divestiture plan for customer negotiation, billing and collection, and service order processes
Customer Premises Equipment Transition Implementation Board	Focal point for managing in 1983 the changes required by the Computer Inquiry II decisions regarding customer premises equipment (CPE), enhanced services, and CPE detariffing
BOC Local Exchange Planning and Implementation Group	BOC advocate in matters relating to divestiture planning
Personnel	
AT&T Personnel Assignment Steering Committee	Overall coordination of personnel assignments
Regional Personnel Assignment Committee (RPAC)	Regional planning and implementation of personnel assignments
Regulatory	
Access Service Implementation Committee	Responsibility for coordination of the access service tariff filings, billing systems, provisioning and capability processes, and Bell–independent telephone company relations
Regulatory Planning Group	Focus on major regulatory issues involved in implementing divestiture

Table 2   Major Divestiture Boards and Committees (*continued*)

Committee	Function
Regulatory Activities Implementation Committee	Focal point for coordination of issues which involve federal and state regulatory factors
Logistics	
BOC Materials Management Implementation Committee	Resolution of assignment of materials-inventory management assets to divested BOCs
Real Estate, Automotive, and Energy Functional Board	Responsibility for disaggregation of real estate, automotive, and energy functions
Public relations	
Divestiture Customer Information Task Force	Develop informational packages on divestiture for customers
Contractual matters	
Intercompany Contract Steering Committee	Responsibility for development, administration, and coordination of all requirements in connection with postdivestiture intercompany contractual agreements
Intercompany Contract Implementation Committee	Monitor, track, and provide status on contract implementation plans
Board of Contract Negotiators	Provide consensus agreement on working drafts of all contractual agreements

planners could possibly have directed. Another feature was the prevalence of operating company people. Throughout the task forces, BOC representatives were present in very considerable strength to express their views on—and to influence—plans and issues. And so in every respect it was admirably Darwinian, evolving to survive and prevail. Fortunately, too, for, as John Segall, quoted in *The Washington Post* of September 13, 1982, reported, "The task before the thousands of AT&T planners almost defies comprehension."

The Restructure Implementation Board

On August 24, 1982, Judge Greene issued his formal approval of the MFJ, contingent upon several major modifications whose intent was to strengthen the position of the BOCs, which would be grouped, it had been decided, in seven regional units. Specifically, the court decision required that the operating companies be allowed into the "Yellow Pages" and terminal equipment businesses. While controversial both within and outside the Bell System, the decision at least provided a greater measure of certainty on which to proceed.

Eight days later, the first meeting of the Restructure Implementation Board was convened. From its inception this body took its place at the top of the divestiture apparatus, in part as a response to the universally acknowledged need for some sort of superordinate administrative agency that could pull it all together.

Perhaps most important among its many functions, it served as a kind of court of next-to-last resort, a forum to which stalemated issues from the discipline-specific committees could be brought for discussion, resolution, or escalation to senior officers. The mere prospect of that last step was, of course, generally productive in getting most issues settled *sine die.*

In typically participative form, the Restructure Implementation Board (inevitably dubbed RIB) was made up of thirty-four departmental executives at AT&T and an officer with divestiture responsibilities from each BOC region. Three members served as cochairmen: I represented AT&T corporate headquarters; Rob Dalziel represented the Bell Operating Companies; and Ken Garrett provided continuity from the earlier BOC Advisory Board formed to coordinate CI-II activities, from which the RIB was adapted.

Meetings were held every other Wednesday morning, from September 1982 to December 7, 1983. (Pearl Harbor Day seemed to some a particularly appropriate finishing touch.) In addition to the RIB members, regular guests and presenters swelled the gatherings to sixty or seventy people. Conference Room C in the Basking Ridge Operational Complex, the usual meeting site, became known as "the RIB cage," owing to its semicircular, tiered seating arrangements. Analysis of the agendas discloses that all the hottest issues were reviewed and debated again and again within this council. The following were those most frequently discussed:

1. Access service

2. Intercompany contracts (for example, for shared facilities)

3. Functional divestiture (the objective of completing divestiture operationally by October 1, 1983 to allow for a shakedown period)

4. Procurement (augmenting the capabilities of the companies to perform procurement functions)

5. Force assignment

6. Embedded base organization (for existing customer equipment in place)

7. Plan of reorganization

8. WATS/800 service (an issue of jurisdiction: Is Wide Area Telephone and 800 Service within a local exchange solely BOC business?)

9. Asset assignment

10. 1984 cash flow requirements

With the passing months, the emotional content of each issue's debate tended to rise in direct proportion to its potential financial or market impact.

The BOC Voice

Many sideliners to divestiture perceived AT&T as the dominant and self-serving partner in sorting out the family jewels. Wrote one Southern state public utility commissioner in *The New York Times* of March 16, 1982: "In one fell swoop [AT&T] used a giant ladle to scoop into a Bell jar the most exciting, profitable and potentially profitable operations of the business, leaving the BOC's with hardly a curd." However, the real management of the unbundling, and the actual functioning of the Restructure Implementation Board, would have borne no resemblance to this entertaining cartoon. The seven BOC representatives who sat on the board, along with their appointed representative, Rob Dalziel, invariably waged a vigorous and potent advocacy on the companies' behalf.

In this regard, Dalziel arranged for alternative Tuesday evening "pre-RIB" meetings, informal gatherings to prepare the BOC members for the more formal Wednesday convocations. These Tuesday sessions must rank among the most intense and provocative of all divestiture deliberations, with impassioned appeals for BOC unity giving place to questions of a subtler shading.

One Tuesday evening, for example, Sam Ginn, executive vice president of Pacific Telephone, asked whether "all business beginning and ending within exchange access boundaries—even 800 and WATS calls—should not belong to the BOCs?" This simple, seemingly innocent query, soliciting collegial support on the allocation of such lucrative services, was gradually to escalate into what may have been the most contentious wrangle in the entire divestiture process. And it was only one of a number of flammable issues first articulated in the pre-RIB discussions.

An interesting anomaly of these meetings was that while their objective was to share strategy and bind the operating companies in common purpose, the AT&T RIB cochairman was nonetheless invited. What might have been an awkward situation—the wolf in the fold—was quickly transformed by the demonstration of trust. Needless to say, the implied covenant was scrupulously honored.

The War Rooms

"Planning is a symptom of disorder," Chairman Brown told the BOC presidents. "When the future seems reasonably predictable, planning goes by another name: 'management.' When times are changing, there are planners everywhere."

In the hot days of August, planners were indeed everywhere, and they were especially sensitive to the "disorder." With the divestiture management process so deliberately unregimented, it became necessary to establish a central location from which to track the paths of its advance. Out of this need grew two "war rooms" located at opposite ends of the Basking Ridge complex (Figures 3 and 4). The first was the Corporate Divestiture Management Center, which housed the project's central intelligence system: a computer console and screen ready to display promptly any section of the massive material related to divestiture. For example, if one wished to survey the official provisions on procurement, a simple command would instantly yield all such references to be found in the MFJ, the CI-II Guidelines, the Divestiture Planning Guidelines, the Plan of Reorganization, and any other relevant document. Called "DART," for Direct Access Retrieval Technique, the system served the participants as a computerized library.

DART was supplemented by wall-mounted, color-coded, key-event schedules and major-issue status reports, inasmuch as the cen-

FIGURE 3.   Corporate Divestiture Management Center.

ter was also the setting for hundreds of meetings associated with divestiture. The activity and the panoply quickly signaled to the passerby that something of consequence was happening here.

The second war room—the Transitional Management Support Center—was devoted to operational divestiture. Its justification was self-evident. Operations, as the central nervous system of the entire enterprise, was so vast, so intricate, and so highly integrated, that the job of tracking and reporting its division and restructuring had to be handled as a separate enterprise.

Managers Larry Mead and Errol Unikel created the second center. Even a quick glance around this bright, busy room provided a sense of both its scope and its energy. Here, charts showing the status of operator services, central office operations, planning and engineering, business office operations support services, and intercompany

FIGURE 4. Transitional Management Support Center.

contracts—to name but a few of the functions monitored—were color-coded in stoplight fashion: green for "go" (on schedule); yellow for "caution" (behind schedule); and red for "danger" (acceptable divestiture in jeopardy).

Managers in this room drew on a vast, Bell System–wide network which relayed objective self-appraisals from far-flung operational units reporting on their monthly progress. Parenthetically, that they should willingly and candidly detail their own problems and delays was consistent with the self-reporting tradition on operational matters that had long been part of the culture and a major contributor to service quality. In effect, this was yet another example of a legacy harnessed to pull its own house down.

The "war rooms" appellation proved to be apt: apt because it reflected the revolution within the Bell System created by the Consent Decree; apt in that the revolution provoked intense struggles between separated factions; apt because the management of the project required many of the techniques and tools associated with military command posts.

It seems remarkable, in retrospect, that the media did not make more of the war rooms. Perhaps the sheer magnitude of efforts there was overwhelming. The few times reporters and researchers did visit, they took copious notes, asked dozens of questions, and shot hundreds of pictures—all of which, apparently, ended up in editors' wastebaskets.

That, however, was of no consequence to the planners. They were too busy to notice.

FOURTH QUARTER, 1982:
THE PLAN OF REORGANIZATION

> Not later than six months after the effective date of Final Judgment, Defendant AT&T shall submit to the Department of Justice, for its approval, and thereafter implement, a plan of reorganization.

So began part A, section I of the Modification of Final Judgment, which was certified by Judge Greene on August 24, 1983. In effect, the Department of Justice had said, "The Bell System will indeed be broken up. Now, AT&T, it is incumbent upon you to tell us how you will accomplish this Herculean task, for us to approve or disapprove." No other reference to the Plan of Reorganization (POR) was to be found anywhere in this astonishingly brief instrument. Consequently, AT&T managers would have to develop the plan without the benefit of specifications, requirements, or even a hint of the scope or content expected by Assistant Attorney General Baxter.

To most of us, it seemed yet another manifestation of the naïveté that many in Washington exhibited—including some who had stalked AT&T most relentlessly—as to the complexities of the project, apart from its consequences. One operating company officer recalled a World War II response to the problems posed by German submarines. "Just heat the ocean to 200 degrees Fahrenheit," a strategist proposed, "and when the subs are forced to surface, our Air Force can sink them." Asked how one manages such a feat, he replied: "It's my job to develop solutions; it's *your* job to implement them."

Initially, many at AT&T assumed that the plan submitted to the Justice Department could be a brief document, paralleling the order that had called it into being. They assumed it could be supported by detailed reference binders at AT&T, cross-indexed to support the plan's general methodology, and so on.

The notion was short-lived. Within days it was recognized that the Plan of Reorganization would become the blueprint from which divestiture would be engineered and constructed. As one participant noted, it would be "the divestiture Bible, Bill of Rights and Constitution all in one." Its precise terms and conditions would be virtually etched in stone for all the world to comment on, object to, argue over, and judge. No more provisional assumption sets would be developed, no more alternative options or definitions. This was it! The Plan of Reorganization would take divestiture public and would in many ways define the telecommunications industry for years to come.

Indeed, what would be delivered to Judge Greene would be a complete and detailed legal document describing how assets would be separated, how employees would be reassigned, how indivisible facilities would be shared, how obligations and liabilities would be honored, and how the rights of all parties would be guaranteed, to name but a few of its official commitments. But that also meant that the general principles derived from the presidential study teams and other deliberative task groups would not suffice; many others would have to be defined to complete the plan.

What's more, they would have to be defined quickly. At the dawning of divestiture's fourth quarter, AT&T's senior management concluded that "six months after the effective date" was too long to wait to submit the plan. That interval, followed by the required 12-month implementation period, would push divestiture to February 24, 1984. Such an awkward date was insupportable, especially in light of financial requirements to balance books of account and develop audit trails in the monumental eight-way separation—an effort that practically demanded a tidier end-of-year basis and treatment.

More by necessity than by critical path planning, January 1, 1984 was set as D-Day (D for divestiture), thus promulgating a rational launching date for each new entity and a clear and workable schedule for literally millions of requisite financial transactions. Immediately, "one-one-eighty-four" was heard in AT&T's corridors and conference rooms like some mystic formula, just as "pee-oh-are" (POR) would take hold a few weeks later, both serving to galvanize activities throughout the year's final quarter.

The POR Cauldron

Working backward from January 1, 1984, a target of November 30, 1982, was set for submission of the Plan of Reorganization (POR) to the Justice Department. Once more, a sense of "mission impossible" prevailed, with 2 months allowed for a 6-month job. Just a few months earlier the board chairman had said that "The future . . . relies on enlisting the participation of employees at all levels who are unafraid to accept new challenges and eager to take advantage of new opportunities." Unquestionably, a new challenge and new opportunity had arrived—in spades—and soon the intensity of the effort summoned was palpable.

First, however, the developmental process may be of more than passing interest to students both of management and of divestiture. As a legal document the POR had to be written by lawyers, interpreted by lawyers, and approved by lawyers. However, its substance comprised complex financial, operational, technical, personnel, and procedural matters, all outside the ken of most attorneys. Furthermore, the plan required the initiation of entirely original management principles in very short order and an internal consistency in the document itself that would stand as an extraordinary editorial feat.

The first step was to devise a table of contents, a task requiring no small degree of creativity, given the lack of specificity in the MFJ. This step yielded a four-part structure that can be condensed as follows:

Part 1 How Bell Operating Company facilities, personnel and books of account would be divided

Part 2 How Bell Operating Companies would receive resources that would enable them to be independent of AT&T

Part 3 Terms and conditions of canceling certain existing internal contractual relationships among elements of the Bell System

Part 4 How assets and liabilities will be restructured among AT&T and the regional companies

---

To observe that the structure was deceptively simple is to understate the case substantially. The POR would have to anticipate every one of literally millions of acts and actions that would proceed from the first tick of the clock on 1/1/84. As Chairman Brown described it to the *Seattle Rotary* on August 25, 1982:

> More than one million employees must follow their jobs, and tens of thousands of them must transfer from one former Bell company to another. Data processing systems must be reprogrammed, reconfigured, and, in some cases, redeployed—systems that control maintenance, repair, and installation work, that generate employees' paychecks and customers' bills, that keep records and manage the large information systems needed to run a giant business. State and federal tariffs establishing prices must be amended and refiled—in perhaps as many as 50 thousand pages of documents. On Day One after divestiture, the former Bell companies must be prepared to process 600 million telephone calls, dispatch 100 thousand installation and repair technicians, and continue a 17.5-billion-dollar modernization program.

The second step in developing the POR was to establish the organization and the process that would erect on the four-part framework the appropriate structure of a workable plan. As the occasion was uncommon, so was the response. The organization formed was essentially a troika consisting of subject matter experts as technical knowledge brokers, lawyers as writers and managing editors, and corporate planners as arbiters and overall coordinators. It was a union born of necessity, a union that would experience considerable strains.

The third step was the subsequent assignment of teams to address each part of the plan's development and subteams to address each subpart. In this effort there were a number of discipline-specific AT&T-BOC groups focused on particular sections of the POR.

As the POR cauldron began to boil, participants came to agree with Goethe that "the greatest difficulties lie where we are not looking for them." The expected difficulties were sufficient unto the day—i.e., in designing the architecture of the plan. But unanticipated and frequently complicating difficulties arose within the troika as the three elements tended to pull in different directions. Of the attorneys, the SMEs' frequent complaint was: "They may know the law, but they don't understand the telephone business." Retorted the lawyers: "The SMEs don't understand the purpose or requirements of the Consent Decree." The planners stood uncomfortably between the two groups, resolved to arbitrate and coordinate, but prepared, when all else failed, to escalate the differences.

In retrospect, the heat sometimes generated may have tempered the principles and decisions that emerged into something more durable. The stakes were high, and the parties grew more conscious of it. Unresolved issues that had been treated gingerly by AT&T staffs and their counterparts in the regional companies suddenly created confrontational incidents and unaccustomed acerbity in relationships that had always reflected the almost inordinately courteous and restrained nature of the culture.

Critical POR Issues

In the second week in October, a first and admittedly preliminary draft of the POR was remitted to the BOCs for comments. The objective was to bring to the surface technical differences and any critical concerns that required attention at the highest managerial levels before the POR could advance further. In a different sense than the recently popular advertising slogan intended, this early draft also asked "Where's the beef?"

The beefs were forthcoming. They emerged in early November in the form of fifteen core issues, each of which would be carried to the very top of the corporation for resolution. A November 4 transmittal memorandum prepared by corporate planning stated: "Attached is a set of (unresolved) issues arising from an analysis of BOC responses to the October 10th initial draft of the Plan of Reorganization. They need prompt resolution if current target dates are to be met."

The density of these issues argues against their detailed development here. However, the designation or subject area of each and the central question each addressed, as demonstrated in Table 3, should help convey their weight.

Inescapably, the positions of each of the eight major entities had to be documented in infinite detail. Corporate planning's Bruce Barr and a hardy band of six assistants sought out precise position statements from all sides for encapsulation in language understandable and useful to senior management—succeeding after weeks of successive 18-hour days, nimble shuttle diplomacy, and intense interpretive work.

Table 3   Critical Plan of Reorganization Issues, November 1982

Issue	Designation	Key questions
1	Employee assignment	In the transfer of employees across corporate boundaries, how will shortages and surpluses be allocated?
2	Directory	Can AT&T retain rights to directory software and systems even though directory operations remain in the BOCs?
3	Customer equipment	Can some customer equipment employees remain in the BOCs even though the operations and equipment are transferred to AT&T?
4	Business use limitations	Can the BOCs use "intelligence" (patents, software, etc.) for business use beyond "exchange and exchange access" as defined in the MFJ?
5	Divestiture cost	How will the enormous cost of divesting the BOCs be allocated among the seven regional holding companies and AT&T?
6	Billing for customer equipment	How will AT&T bill for the 70 million customer equipment accounts transferred to it on January 1, 1984?

Table 3   Critical Plan of Reorganization Issues, November 1982 (*continued*)

Issue	Designation	Key questions
7	Inside-wire asset assignment	Should wiring for complex customer business systems be transferred to AT&T? (The MFJ called for all inside wire to remain with the BOCs.)
8	Procurement	What material and personnel must be transferred from Western Electric to the BOCs to enable them to perform procurement functions after January 1, 1984?
9	Central office switches located on customer premises	Should these switches be classified as customer PBXs (and transferred to AT&T) or as local exchange switches (and remain with the BOCs)?
10	Business information systems and software developed at AT&T, Bell Labs, Western Electric	How will the systems and supporting personnel be divided and transferred to BOCs?
11	Telephone equipment serving BOCs	Should this be transferred to AT&T or remain in the operating companies?
12	Bell name and logo	Who retains rights to use the Bell name and logo?
13	Central staff commitment period	Should the BOC right to withdraw support be set at 10 years or 5 years from January 1, 1984 (that is, the central staff, now known as Bell Communications Research, that would be established to serve the regional companies)?
14	Central staff funding	How should the BOC central staff be funded? (AT&T not involved)
15	Calling cards (long-distance credit cards)	Who will issue credit cards after divestiture: AT&T, the BOCs, or both?

Remarkably, each issue had at its root one common theme: deep concern over the financial condition of the postdivestiture companies. Equally remarkable was that in not one case did the actors have a precise assessment of the financial impact of winning or losing the issue at hand; they were dividing the silver in this corporate divorce without knowing what it was actually worth. Still, the arguments were often acrimonious, although it is difficult to ascertain, in retrospect, how much of the emotion flared from anger over the breakup, and how much was in defense of sound financial considerations. Certainly, given the pervasive uncertainties, it would have been unnatural for the designated chief executive officers and their staffs to concede any substantive point without at least a skirmish.

As each of the issues was argued and as portions of each began to be resolved, the dissolution of the Bell System slipped at least temporarily from page 1 of the nation's press. The POR was confusing and made for less-than-exciting reading, especially at a time when the public's imagination was engaged with the dramatic hunt for the Tylenol killer and the stubborn Milwaukee Brewers were stretching the World Series to seven games before yielding finally to the St. Louis Cardinals.

However, the growing dissension among Bell entities was no less dramatic to top management at AT&T. Their concern led them to focus even more sharply on the divestiture project. On November 1 AT&T Vice President William G. Sharwell was appointed as the officer responsible for overall divestiture activities, releasing John Segall to devote full attention to the extraordinary challenge of planning and financial management for the new AT&T. Sharwell, a broad-gauged, practical, and seasoned executive, had helped to see the New York Telephone Company through its severe service crisis in the late 1960s, a pressure-laden experience that would stand him in good stead in discharging his new duties.

Only 4 days into the new job, Sharwell received the critical-issues memorandum and forwarded it with comments to the board chairman. The timing was perfect; the fall Presidents' Conference was scheduled for the following week and would provide an extraordinary opportunity for Chairman Brown to work through the remaining critical issues with each of the designated chief executive officers. (In fact, with the deadline for submission of the POR only a few weeks away, these summit discussions might prove to be as important as any others in the divestiture proceedings.)

However, the unsettled items intensified a growing awareness among the eight CEO designates (seven regions plus central staff) of the combined magnitude and yet unfixed nature of their new responsibilities. Set against the clear intent of AT&T officers to command the divestiture tiller, it contributed to a growing sense of uneasiness among them even as they made final preparations to convene.

Fall 1982 Presidents' Conference

Not unexpectedly, the entire conference was given over to divestiture, with the Plan of Reorganization, financial implications of separation, and implementation activities the targeted areas of concentration. With respect to overall management of divestiture, three segments of the conference were aimed at moving the process forward.

First, Bill Sharwell provided a thorough briefing on where things stood. He reported that the divestiture apparatus was fully in place, and ticked off the major milestone dates that would have to be achieved. He also described the organizational goals: "Divestiture, then, is a zero-sum game organizationally. Collectively, we must come out even." And he concluded with a combined appeal and admonition: "It is essential that we continue to collaborate."

Sharwell was followed by AT&T's charismatic president, William M. Ellinghaus, who continued the essential theme of collaboration into the second conference segment. Ellinghaus, a self-made executive who enjoyed considerable credibility with operating company presidents, sought to ameliorate the growing tensions among colleagues who soon would be competitors.

The precise message Ellinghaus delivered that day was never reported. However, excerpts from his prepared notes stated:

- As we drive toward specificity in settling disputes on these matters (issues), there is enormous potential for emotional polarization.
- The soundest basis for our collective judgements is . . . what serves the best interests of our constituencies, our mutual shareholders, our mutual customers and our employees.
- In this way we can deal with divestiture in a fashion that does credit to our heritage, in a climate that is rational, temperate, productive.
- If, on any issue, you feel you are not getting even-handed treatment, pick up the telephone and call me. I cannot guarantee assent, but I can guarantee a fair hearing.

It was a statesmanlike offer, one that would be accepted more than once in the remaining 13½ months until 1/1/84.

After the presentations, the chairman met with the eight CEO designates to thrash out the remaining POR concerns. It could have been done no other way. The issues had been "staffed out," analyzed in prodigious detail, reviewed by the RIB, negotiated interminably by lawyers and staff executives, and still wanted resolution. The Fall Conference was the last stop before Washington, D.C.

The discussions were frank, intense, but completely controlled. Compromises were sought and, on several issues, attained. Others eventuated in impasse and would have to be settled in Washington. That is to say, the POR as submitted to the Department of Justice would embody the AT&T position. It was, after all, the legal responsibility of the owner, AT&T, to interpret and execute the terms of the MFJ. However, the divested companies did have recourse, in the form of sworn affidavits submitted to the Justice Department with the POR, spelling out the underlying reasons for objections. AT&T submitted its contrasting views in the affidavit format as well.

The Submission

In the early morning hours of December 16, a handful of AT&T legal staff members waited at the printers. Complicated by repeated last-minute changes, production of the 471-page POR had been delayed again and again. Now, finally, the first copies were bound and packed into thirty boxes, which were rushed to LaGuardia Airport for a shuttle flight to Washington. Before departure, one copy was signed by Chairman Brown, and this was hand carried to the court.

In all, 10,000 copies were printed. As anticipated, the work fell somewhat short of *War and Peace* in several categories. Nonetheless, copies were eagerly sought. Only minutes after Judge Greene received his copy, Bill Sharwell's was delivered to him at Basking Ridge. Within the hour, dozens more were being distributed to key management personnel at AT&T, including RIB and DPG members. By midmorning, hundreds were being provided to members of Congress and the media, and before nightfall, 150 more were mailed first-class to all "active parties" (that is, intervenors) to the case. For months the industry, regulators, law firms, financial analysts, legislators, and business schools deluged the distribution center at AT&T's

Piscataway, New Jersey, facility with requests that soon depleted supplies.

The plan was a far cry from the original conception of a brief instrument outlining general schemes and intent. Still, as Chairman Brown noted in the *AT&T Management Report* of December 17, 1982, "It is not an exhaustive enumeration of the divestiture process. Rather it is a precise blueprint—a road map—describing as comprehensively as possible how we intend to conform with the decree."

Three major elements of that process were announced for the first time in the plan: the financial arrangements whereby AT&T would launch the companies with the debt ratios specified in the Modification of Final Judgment, the specific stock ownership and transfer provisions, and the particulars on the division of assets.

With regard to financial arrangements, the regional companies would be assigned 75 percent of AT&T's total assets of $140 to $150 billion. To divest the companies with a 45 percent debt ratio (50 percent for Pacific Telephone), AT&T pledged to assume some of their interest and principal payments on long-term debt and, if necessary, to write off some of the $1 billion in short-term advances it had loaned them.

On stock ownership, the plan called for stockholders to receive one share of common stock in each of the seven newly created regional companies for every ten shares of AT&T stock owned as of a record date in December 1983. Shares in the regional companies would be in addition to the AT&T shares investors already owned. Because more than 100 million shareholder transactions were expected to be processed for the regional companies and AT&T during 1984—and because an unprecedented 22 million shareholder accounts would exist at divestiture—AT&T would set up and operate a wholly owned subsidiary to provide a full range of record-keeping and other shareholder services for its own use and, on a fee basis, for the regional companies. Shares of the regional companies would begin to be traded on a "when issued" basis in November or December 1983, even before divestiture took effect.

The plan further specified that the division of Bell System assets—from multimillion-dollar electronic switchers down to vans and cars—would be based on the principle of sole or predominant use. For example, transmission, switching, and plant facilities, including cables, poles, buildings, motor vehicles, office equipment and furniture, would be assigned to an operating company or to AT&T according to which entity used them more. Where equipment and facilities are shared by the local exchange and interexchange users, ownership would be assigned to the predominant user, who would be allowed to lease to the other, for a limited time, the needed equipment or facilities.

Assignment of personnel to either AT&T or operating company units would generally be guided by the principle that employees follow their work. Basing assignments on job functions would minimize job relocation and employee inconvenience. Accordingly, the vast majority of Bell System people would remain in their current jobs with their current companies. Other employees would change companies but would generally be able to remain in their current job locations and continue their current work.

Thus, to the degree possible, the eventual divestiture would proceed according to the vision of balanced responsibilities that Bill Ellinghaus had invoked. A 1982 issue of *Bell Telephone Magazine* confirmed this vision in reporting how the plan specified

> . . . that service will be provided at the same or better levels than have been the Bell System's hallmark; that the integrity of the investment of AT&T's 3.2 million share owners will be preserved; that employment security and continued career opportunity will be ensured; and that the divested companies will be launched with all the management, financial, technical, and physical resources necessary to help them flourish in the regions where they will operate.

Commenting from his own vantage, Chairman Brown declared in the *AT&T Management Report* of December 27, 1982: "I am not so naïve as to think every detail of the Plan will be greeted with unanimous acclaim. There will be critics whose special interests will prompt them to seek special advantage at the expense of the Bell Companies and their share owners." And he added: "One final point: don't let anyone convince you that this plan was something 'dictated' to the Bell Operating Companies by AT&T. There was consultation with the companies, and compromise. The document represents a collaboration, not a single exercise of anyone's will."

The Affidavits

Two days before the POR was submitted to the Department of Justice, *The Wall Street Journal* featured an article headlined, "AT&T Is

Fought by Pacific Unit on Divestiture." It related Pacific's eleventh hour effort—a successful one—to seek a lower debit ratio than prescribed in the POR because of its weaker financial position. Interestingly, the article referred to the dispute as the "first intramural split." In fact, it was merely the first to reach the media's attention. As noted, contention was hardly unknown throughout this period; by common consent and tradition, it had simply been kept within doors.

Of the original fifteen issues listed previously, eight had been settled. Positions on the remaining seven, together with an additional eleven, were conveyed in affidavits submitted with the plan. Table 4 (page 60) summarizes the issues addressed in those affidavits, thus providing a guide to the significant matters remaining unresolved at the midpoint of the divestiture planning process.

With the submission of the POR, these issues lingered before the Justice Department and Judge Greene. Many would not be laid to rest until the court's final approval on August 5, 1983. Even thereafter, questions of the plan's interpretation and intent would arise on a regular basis, serving to sustain the flames of controversy that were fanned from sparks struck during 1982's planning phases. One example was WATS and 800 services, a dispute that stretched throughout 1983 and beyond as the parties sought out their strongest possible market positions in their new competitive worlds. Still, the questions were few, whereas thousands of other difficult agreements and accommodations had been concluded satisfactorily—the thousands that made a successful divestiture possible.

At this point, a logical question might be: From a managerial standpoint, how did the decision process work to deal with the hundreds of complex and controversial causes? And the answer: By means of the organizational hierarchy. But then one might wonder if this implied a miracle of modern managerial techniques. Hardly. In fact, the process is as old as the Bible, wherein it states in Exodus 18:25–26:

> And Moses chose able men out of all Israel, and made them heads over the people, rulers of thousands, rulers of hundreds, rulers of fifties, and rulers of tens.
>
> And they judged the people at all seasons: the hard causes they brought unto Moses, but every small matter they judged themselves.

It just has to be added that in the context of divestiture, small matters could often be sizable in proportion.

Table 4 Remaining POR Issues

Issue	Regions commenting	Final settlement
Inside-wire asset assignment	US West, Pacific Telesis, NYNEX, Southwestern Bell	Inside wire assigned to BOCs
Non-ESS software rights	US West, Pacific Telesis, Southwestern Bell	Non-ESS (electronic switching system) software rights determined according to a categorization scheme
Allocation of contingent liabilities	US West, Pacific Telesis, Southwestern Bell	Contingent liabilities are a shared responsibility of AT&T and BOCs, based on assignment of assets
Western Electric services procurement	US West, Pacific Telesis, Southwestern Bell	Western Electric procurement resource allocation concerns jointly resolved during implementation phase
Directory operations and related support systems	US West, Ameritech, Southwestern Bell	Both BOCs and AT&T have discrete rights to directory system software
Charge-a-call ownership	US West, Ameritech, Southwestern Bell	Charge-a-call assigned to BOCs

Assignment of multifunction buildings	U S West, Pacific Telesis, Southwestern Bell	"Predominant use" theory was slightly modified to accommodate some technical complexities
Contract flexibility	Pacific Telesis, Southwestern Bell, Ameritech	BOCs and AT&T codified their contract concerns in series of principal divestiture agreements
Pension fund actuarial	U S West, Pacific Telesis	BOCs selected their own actuaries
Calling card ownership	U S West, Pacific Telesis	Both BOCs and AT&T offer calling card services
Intellectual properties (trademarks, trade names)	U S West, Pacific Telesis	"Bell" name assigned to BOCs, although AT&T may continue to use "Bell Laboratories"
Business use limitations	Southwestern Bell	Use of certain facilities in accordance with approved plan
Assignment of official inter-LATA (Local Access and Transport Area) facilities	Pacific Telesis	These facilities were assigned to AT&T

61

Table 4 Remaining POR Issues (*continued*)

Issue	Regions commenting	Final settlement
Debt ratios	Southwestern Bell, Ameritech	Debt ratios for all regions except Pacific were at or below 45%; Pacific was less than 50%, as agreed
Relations with independent telephone companies	U S West	Independent telephone company relationships were worked out with independents during implementation phase
Capital structure and financing	Pacific Telesis	Level of short-term debt was not quantified and preferred stock was not treated as debt
Pacific remand tax financing	Pacific Telesis	Pacific resolved this issue through agreements with government authorities
National security centralized staff, single point of contact	Southwestern Bell	Bell Communications Research, Inc. provides national security centralized single point of contact

FIRST QUARTER 1983: FROM PLAN TO IMPLEMENTATION

With the Plan of Reorganization filed, the numerous planning issues at last decided, and a well-deserved Christmas vacation behind them, Bell System managers turned their collective attention to implementing divestiture.

1982 had witnessed a frenetic effort—especially at AT&T, but with extensive BOC involvement—to develop the plan. 1983 loomed no less frenetic, but now the challenge would be to make the plan happen, and the pressure for responding would shift more toward the managements of the BOCs. The coincidental timing of the new phase with the new year accentuated the sharp change in focus of the divestiture effort. With the onset of implementation, there would be a significant increase in specialization—a diffusion of thousands of details.

Each detail, each responsibility, each predictable event would have to be documented and planned. Tracking reports had indicated that although consciousness of divestiture was ubiquitous, a great need still existed throughout the Bell System for a comprehensive explication of the effort still ahead. Consequently, a second set of divestiture guidelines was developed and issued to the Bell Operating Companies, Long Lines, and Western Electric.

Just as the 1982 planning guidelines had provided a blueprint for the prior year's planning effort, this set spelled out, on a function-by-function basis, the thousands of activities, assumptions, assignments of responsibility, and timeframes that would be required in 1983 in the interest of an orderly transition.

Three examples:

- On 1/1/84, the AT&T Cellular Services Subsidiaries will be divested to the BOCs. At the same time, all construction permits and approved radio licenses will be transferred.

- Determination of predominant use for purposes of building investment will be based on quantities of floor space occupied.

- Minicomputers that perform functions for the BOCs, such as COSMOS, will be assigned to the BOCs.

Now, armed not only with the principles set forth in the POR but also with meticulous instructions as to how those principles should be implemented, the entire Bell System could move forward on a broad front. While it was still virtually impossible to comprehend the task in its totality, the collective efforts of thousands of specialists— each laboring in his or her own figurative vineyard—would together achieve it nonetheless. Said a different way, the campaign had been mapped and planned in detail; now it devolved upon the field commanders and troops in the trenches to carry the day.

Internal Milestones

In keeping with the broad implementation agenda depicted in the divestiture guidelines, a series of noteworthy milestones in the inexorable march toward divestiture was being reached. For example, by FCC mandate American Bell Incorporated (later AT&T Information Systems) was inauguarated on January 1, 1983, to market, sell, and maintain *newly* manufactured equipment and enhanced services.

It was an auspicious inauguration indeed. As *The New York Times* noted on January 3, 1983: "High-technology companies often start with a few people working in a garage. American Bell Inc. will open for business today with 28,000 employees working in 700 buildings. Such a grand beginning is appropriate for a company that is opening a new era of competition in the telephone business."

However, even as it celebrated the launching of what headline writers liked to call "Baby Bell," AT&T was hoping against hope that the FCC would allow the deregulation of embedded customer premises equipment (CPE), the 70 million telephones and thousands of PBX and key systems in use throughout the country, equipment that would be transferred to AT&T at divestiture. As noted previously, the prospect of providing customer equipment and services in a bifurcated, or two-mode manner, was appalling to telephone people. Furthermore, the uncertain regulatory status of CPE, an uncertainty that was to persist until the eleventh hour, played havoc with divestiture planning efforts.

Another milestone in the first quarter was the remarkable achievement of a shared-network agreement between Long Lines and the BOCs. The complicated and sensitive task of determining how the ownership of inseparable switching and transmission equipment would be apportioned—and what the "sharing" arrangements concluded after separation would be—was the Gordian knot of divestiture. From the moment the MFJ was signed, this had been a central concern for Bell management. Thus its resolution brought a special sigh of relief.

Other milestones were announced almost weekly, including a trial in Southern Bell to test principles for the division of assets; the initial redeployment of AT&T headquarters units; the sale to customers for the first time of in-place CPE under tariffs; and the finalization of plans for the Central Services Organization (later to be named Bell Communications Research).

In years past any of these milestones would have represented an event of cosmic proportions within the corporation. But in the divestiture maelstrom, they were taken in stride—important, of course, but seen essentially as only the latest of hundreds of steps toward the larger goal at year's end.

External Milestones

Outside the Bell System, a corresponding stream of changes occurred in early 1983, with each incident adding to the overall divestiture mosaic. For example, despite some strident claims to the contrary, the Supreme Court affirmed in February that the MFJ Consent Decree was in the public interest and thus closed the book on the nation's most complex antitrust case. As a *Bell Telephone Magazine* of 1983 reported, "In describing its position on an agreement that took eight years to make, the court used only four words: 'The judgment is affirmed.' It was the right decision, both for AT&T and the nation, for given all that had gone before, backtracking would have been virtually impossible."

Also in February, the FCC ordered that access tariffs, the charges the divested companies would levy on the long distance companies for local connections to customers, be filed by January 1, 1984. The structure and level of these charges, perhaps the central issue in all of divestiture, would continue to be debated within the Bell System, among industry protagonists, and in regulatory and political arenas through 1983 and beyond. The extent and fervor of that controversy reflected its importance to the future financial fortunes of each of the emerging telecommunications entities.

In the financial community, Moody's Investors Service delivered a shock by downgrading the bond ratings of virtually every Bell company, including AT&T and Western Electric. Claiming that divestiture posed a greater credit risk, Moody's lowered AT&T's senior debt a notch to double-A-1, downgraded sixteen other Bell units by three or more levels, and cut two companies—Chesapeake & Potomac of West Virginia and Michigan Bell—six levels, from triple-A to single-A-3. Bill Cashel, AT&T's chief financial officer, responded: "These are harsh ratings not borne out by the facts. For the most part, the financial position of Bell companies has been improving, not deteriorating. Interest coverage is better. Debt ratios have been reduced significantly." Four days later, as if to confirm Cashel's view, newspapers reported that AT&T topped the buy list of the nation's institutional investors during the fourth quarter of 1982, and banks, brokers, insurance companies, and pension funds increased their AT&T holdings by $819 million. Two weeks later, Standard & Poor's issued stronger ratings for AT&T—ratings that were, in Cashel's words, "more realistic."

On the Washington front, AT&T and the Justice Department agreed to twelve amendments to the POR, essentially as a result of comments from fifty-one intervenors. Notable among the changes was the assignment of the Bell name and logo to the regional companies, a considerable concession. The original plan proposed that both AT&T and the separated operating companies use the Bell trademarks. However, as *Business Week* noted on January 4, 1983, "some independent telephone makers—such as Tandy Corp., whose Radio Shack Division is the largest retail seller of telephones—vowed to fight that." Clearly, it was a fight the intervenors won.

Other amendments assigned noncoin charge-a-call telephones to the regionals and granted the operating companies the right to sublicense certain patents directly. These, too, were far from trivial concessions, reached only after extensive deliberations and gut-wrenching compromise. However, they served to end all remaining disputes between the company and the government over the plan and thus constituted especially critical events in the schedule of divestiture.

Divestiture Implementation Assessment

"The task he undertakes," Shakespeare wrote in *King Richard II*, "is numbering sands and drinking oceans dry." Despite the crescendo of guidelines, organizational adjustments, and both internal and external milestone events, a collective nervousness began to be felt at AT&T, an apprehensiveness derived from confronting the question: Can we—and can they—possibly complete all that must be done this year to divest on 1/1/84? One AT&T observer noted, "Last year at this time the planning ball was in our court, and the BOCs were nervous about our ability to devise the plan. This year the implementation ball's in their court, and we're worried whether they can pull it off."

Under the best of circumstances, the myriad activities awaiting attention would justify feelings of discomfort on both sides of the net. Not surprisingly, those feelings were intensified as certain trouble areas began to slow the pace. In the western United States, for example, there were problems in resolving where AT&T's points of presence would be established—that is, the jointly agreed-upon locations where AT&T and BOC facilities would meet. Ultimately, these problems could delay asset ownership assignments at particular sites, thus potentially swelling the downstream delays in the critical asset assignment area.

Further, several critical-path projects were known to be on a shaky course, and senior Bell managers suspected that other aspects of the overall implementation might be lagging as well. What was needed was a candid assessment of each region's status so that problem areas and threatened schedules could be addressed early in the implementation phase; discovering them later might be too late for correction.

A sense of the concern prevailing during that period was clearly reflected in a memorandum I wrote to Bill Sharwell. That memo, written to recommend such an assessment, noted:

A greater number of fragments [exist] as new implementation committees are formed.

Despite all the planning . . . actual implementation will be a tremendous shock to the companies.

An increasing potential [exists] for a more adversarial relationship between AT&T and the divested companies.

Discernible trends are emerging that work against our effort to keep everything on track.

Accordingly, on March 17, Bill Sharwell recommended to an assemblage of Bell System senior management that a divestiture implementation assessment program begin immediately. Ten major activities—access services, contracts, billing and collecting, service provisioning, force assignment, maintenance, procurement, asset assignment, regulatory, and CPE transition—would be assessed in each region, each in relationship to current schedules. Also, problems of any kind, whether internal (for example, insufficient resources) or external (for example, regulatory lag in decisions) would be brought to the surface and addressed.

Presenting such a recommendation at this point in the divestiture process was a delicate matter, to be sure. The growing feelings of independence within regional managements led some to speculate that such a proposal from AT&T would raise eyebrows, if not hackles. Fortunately, the recognition that "we're all in this together" combined with the infinitely logical realization that whatever the difficulties and delays might be, it would be better to know about them sooner than later. Thus the proposal was embraced by the regional chief executive officers. At the same time, the second quarter's work was cut out for the divestiture planning staff and for those at AT&T and in the regions responsible for each of the ten projects that had been targeted for assessment.

Throughout the first quarter of 1983, the public had been buffeted by confusing, often conflicting projections of AT&T and the prospective telecommunications environment beyond divestiture. Some reassuring overview, it seemed, would serve all parties well.

Picking up *The Wall Street Journal* on February 28, 1983, I found just such an overview in an AT&T advertisement signed by Chairman Brown. A few of its phrases seemed especially relevant to the efforts and expectations within the Bell System:

> We're adapting our business to what the public expects. We have the engineering and scientific resources. And we have our pride. The Bell System as we now know it will be no more. We will divest. But we are not demolishing the promise of tomorrow. That promise is alive and well. Bell System people are ready for new directions.

SECOND QUARTER, 1983: THE ASSESSMENT PROCESS

"Quite as important as legislation," Woodrow Wilson wrote, "is vigilant oversight of administration." Indeed, there was a considerable sense of the wisdom of this observation in the first days of divestiture's second spring. The figurative legislation of divestiture was well-documented; now, the conscientious pursuit of the all-important divestiture implementation assessment program would constitute the vigilant oversight of its administration.

The program consisted essentially of two steps. The first was completion by each region, Western Electric, and AT&T Long Lines, of detailed questionnaires designed by AT&T to gauge progress in each of the ten critical areas targeted by Bell senior management on March 17. These asked for assessments of the current resources (e.g., staff, software, management commitment) being employed to meet schedules, and of the external constraints (e.g., legal, regulatory, union) affecting schedules. In addition, and perhaps most notable, they asked for an overall judgment as to whether the project was in serious jeopardy of failing the 1/1/84 deadline.

The second step was a mid-April series of region-by-region meetings between AT&T, BOC, and Western Electric officers that would focus on trouble areas in each region, to discover what local plans were afoot to solve any problems that were soluble at that level, and to ascertain how the considerable staff resources at AT&T might be utilized to help in resolving those that proved more resistant.

The AT&T team, armed with detailed analyses of responses to the questionnaires, consisted of the Restructure Implementation Board cochairmen (Rob Dalziel and me) and Larry Mead, overseer of the operational aspects of divestiture. Together, we conducted a whirlwind tour of assessment meetings—seven meetings in seven cities in eight days—virtually from one end of the nation to the other.

As we assembled in New York Telephone headquarters at 1095 Avenue of the Americas for the first of those meetings, it struck me that our mission was not unlike final evaluations of military plans before an invasion, or perhaps the extended countdown of a space mission. The seriousness and businesslike demeanor of the seven meetings tended to confirm this feeling. While the host companies were entirely polite, the "good old days" of banter and easy camaraderie were clearly gone—another palpable reminder of the transforming changes in the traditional Bell System culture. Nonetheless, the good news from that first meeting forward was that everyone was cooperating, even if more out of apprehension than brotherhood.

As might be expected, the regional divestiture officers and their teams of subject-matter experts were well-prepared to discuss each of the ten target areas. As these discussions progressed, an ever deeper and richer understanding of the difficulties of separation emerged, an understanding that may have been the most valuable byproduct of the meetings. The division and partial duplication of 200 million customer accounts, the development of a computerized system for billing access charges, negotiating scores of contracts between divested parties, and identifying where every dollar of the $150 billion in assets would go took on a stark new reality. Not surprisingly, that new reality reinforced the critical necessity for strong, persistent, and reciprocal relationships between staffs if all the pieces were to function well after divestiture. To paraphrase George Farquhar, "Necessity was the mother of cooperation."

The Assessment Results

It would have been good news indeed if the assessments could have laid apprehensions to rest. This was not the case. The findings in some areas reinforced and even heightened managerial misgivings.

Not surprisingly, there were differences of opinion about the prospects for on-time development of a procurement capability in the companies, with adequate software to deal with multiple vendors. Others voiced concerns about identifying and administering payroll changes in transferring thousands of people to AT&T. A third group had grave doubts about achieving adequate service provisioning arrangements by divestiture's deadline date.

Nonetheless, overarching concerns were discernible even midway through the series of meetings. In fact, our systematic analyses confirmed a pattern of three trouble spots—access service, contracts, and billing systems—that were of sufficient moment to require escalation to the top of the house. Thus, the decision was made to report our findings to the assembly of Bell's senior management at the Spring Presidents' Conference scheduled for La Quinta, California, a week later.

Interestingly, that venerable institution—the Bell System Presidents' Conference—was, for the first time, split into two sequential sections: 2 days for combined AT&T and BOC officers, and 3 days for the "new AT&T" officers only. The conference theme, "Aiming at 1/1/84—and Beyond," was a useful, if unintended context for introducing the problems threatening the deadline.

In the opening session of the first day, Bill Sharwell told the assembled AT&T officers and regional CEO designates:

> The total divestiture project is seen as having serious problems. Three projects—Access Service, Contracts (between RHCs and AT&T), and Billing Systems—are major contributors to that assessment. Uniformly across regions, these three projects are viewed as having serious problems. Thus . . . the total divestiture effort is approaching a "red" condition.
>
> In addition, several regions have experienced serious concern about procurement and force assignment.
>
> Access service records conversion is in jeopardy. Our view shows a shortage of 1,000 people working on this. Only the BOCs can solve the problem.

Sharwell went on to explain the problems in negotiating contracts for billing between the fragmented companies and with independent telephone companies and the concern with developing adequate procurement capabilities in the divested entities. (Not insignificantly, the latter capability was spelled out clearly as a requirement in the Plan of Reorganization.)

Appropriate recommendations were then presented, to include (1) reexamining plans for access service records conversion, (2) appointing representatives to spearhead contract efforts, and (3) assuring that procurement development proceed at full speed.

Sharwell also exhorted the assembled group to begin realigning operations as if divestiture would be effective on October 1, 1983, rather than 1/1/84. This operational realignment, referred to by some as a "pregame scrimmage," would later take on the name "Functional Divestiture" and would preoccupy—and considerably complicate—AT&T's mainstream efforts in the latter half of the year.

Finally, Sharwell made a plea for collective leadership. "We are at the point in time," he said, "to acknowledge the anxieties of our divestiture implementation managers and be responsive to their leadership needs." Had he been so inclined, he might have recalled Benjamin Franklin's statement to John Hancock on signing the Declaration of Independence: "We must all hang together, or assuredly we shall all hang separately."

Cavalcade of Action

Even as the mainstream assessment activity was being carried out, a steady drumbeat of divestiture-related actions began to quicken the pace of the overall project. For example, AT&T's Jim Olson announced a complete restructuring of AT&T Technologies (see Chapter 3), and AT&T began to develop its postdivestiture management structure and modus operandi. In addition, the sale was announced of the marvelous old headquarters building at 195 Broadway in New York—a symbolic and, to some, poignant reminder of the passage from the old Bell System to the new AT&T.

On April 20, Chairman Brown introduced the seven CEO designates to 2661 shareholders assembled in Atlanta, Georgia, for the annual meeting. "These men will be running the organizations; they will represent three-fourths of your investment," he said. With regard to divestiture, the chairman told his audience that the extreme changes were bound to raise questions about their investment and about the future cost of telephone service. While giving no guarantees, Mr. Brown expressed optimism on both counts.

Meanwhile, costs of local telephone service were very much in the news, to the considerable discomfort of consumers and owners alike. For example, in early April, Manhattan Borough President Andrew Stein warned that, "the breakup of AT&T will raise local telephone rates by an average of almost 50 percent, making phone service a plaything of the rich." Warnings from other quarters were no less dire. "The American public faces the prospect of billions of dollars in local telephone rate increases as phone companies attempt to shift a greater share of their costs to consumers," noted *The Washington Post* of May 16, 1983. "This could be the biggest consumer issue for the rest of the decade," Representative Dan Glickman (D-Kansas) told *Business Week* on June 13, 1983. "Public outcry will likely revolve around the cost of local service, which is expected to rise anywhere from 200% to 400% in the next few years." Indeed, some observers predicted that the phone rate issue would spill over into the congressional and presidential elections in 1984; one even suggested that a powerful single-issue presidential campaign could possibly be made of reuniting the soon-to-be-sundered telephone company.

On the Washington front, the FCC gave tentative support to AT&T's plea to deregulate in-place customer equipment in homes and workplaces, thus giving hope that the preposterous notion of bifurcation would soon be ended. ("Tentative," however, was still no guarantee, and Bell planners were to remain nervous until final approval was forthcoming.)

In the District Court in Washington, Judge Greene essentially approved the Bell System scheme for geographic boundaries between the divested companies and AT&T, the so-called Local Access and Transport Areas (LATAs).

At the midpoint in 1983, the mosaic pieced out by these kinds of actions began to shape the perception that external uncertainties would, indeed, be resolved in time, even if incrementally. In fact, events increasingly seemed to inspire confidence in Bell units on both sides of divestiture. In June, William L. Mobraaten, chief financial officer of the still-unnamed holding company that would include New Jersey Bell, told AT&T shareholders: "We will be, on that first day, one of the 50 largest companies in the country. We're going to be healthy and full of life on day one."

Within AT&T, a similar sense of strength and renewal began to surface, together with a quickened impression of enterprise and opportunity. Aptly, this was the key note Chairman Brown had sounded in his opening remarks at La Quinta.

AT&T was, he pointed out,

A new enterprise which will carry forward and build upon the character, the traditions, the achievements which Bell's invention, Vail's master plan and the Morgan group's money launched on a mission which proved so ambitious that its ultimate achievement—nearly a century later—came to be regarded by government authorities as an intolerable *overachievement.*

And thus it is that today we begin anew, with a new dream in prospect, with a new mission in prospect, with a new dream and a new vision.

There was, of course, much to be done before this vision could begin to be realized. For the remaining months of 1983, the problems uncovered in the April assessment would comprise much of the work to be done at AT&T; and functional divestiture, the simulation modality mentioned earlier, would be the instrument to concentrate and program the schedule of events.

The urgent nature of this effort was reflected in an AT&T planning letter addressed to all Bell Company presidents. The letter advised:

It is imperative that we proceed vigorously to transform how we provide service today into a post-divestiture operating mode to insure an
orderly transition from both the corporation's and the customer's perspective. . . .

Our obligation is to have this massive operational realignment phase
completed by October 1st. . . .

The scope includes all operations personnel, centers, and systems as
well as key staff support units.

Thus the alarm to "predivest" had been rung and, in one manager's analogy, the fire department was leaving the station in
response. Whether or not the operational fires could be extinguished
by 1/1/84 would depend on divestiture's last two quarters.

THIRD QUARTER, 1983: BELL'S ACHILLES' HEEL

Of the several significant paradoxes of divestiture, one of the starkest
made itself manifest during the summer of 1983, as the Bell System's
greatest traditional strength suddenly became its Achilles' heel,
threatening not only the divestiture schedule but the entire divestiture plan. That strength was the highly integrated nature of Bell's vast
operational support systems throughout the nation.

For the better part of a century, consonant with its goal of universal service, AT&T had pursued a policy of singular "one-stop
shopping" for its tens of millions of customers. Behind that policy
lay an effort involving millions of worker-hours and billions of dollars
in expenditures, all focused on the integration and computerization
of operational support systems.

Just as doctors and astronauts require logistical support personnel behind them, every customer contact representative had a host of
supporting technicians, clerical people, and administrative experts
in the wings. Business office representatives, billing personnel,
installation workers, training experts, and myriad engineers were all
interlinked in the provision of telephone service. Tied together by a
network of computerized systems and common data bases, they handled the lion's share of the nation's daily demand for service.

Of course, the designers of these systems never contemplated a
governmental mandate that would require splitting programs arbi-

trarily between long-distance and local calling, and between the provision of home and office equipment and the wire connecting such equipment to the local switch. Hence, no measures had ever been established for such divisions.

Throughout 1982 and the first two quarters of 1983, it had become patently evident that people could be divided between the fragmented companies, albeit with considerable inconvenience; that assets could be apportioned fairly; that new holding companies could be chartered and organized; that even corporate cultures could begin to be consciously modified. But to sunder scores of computer programs, huge data bases, and all the procedures attendant on such systems—while keeping all the parts functioning smoothly and assuring that all their pieces and subdivisions would be separated and fully operational by January 1—loomed as the most difficult task of divestiture. Hence, the uncomfortable aptness of the Achilles' heel analogy.

Accordingly, some felt that operational divestiture would require 3 to 5 years to effect. In fact, it was the tenacious cohesiveness of systems that prompted Sam Ford, an experienced New Jersey Bell executive, to utter his oft-quoted simile: "Divestiture is more like pulling taffy apart then breaking a cookie eight ways."

Indeed, the taffy could not be pulled apart in the allotted time frame, and acknowledgment of this induced compromises: where systems could not be separated or "cloned," a sharing clause in the Consent Decree would be invoked. The "owner" of the system would provide service to the "client" until such time after divestiture as new systems could be developed. Soon, 70 million customers would receive physical confirmation of this arrangement in the mails: split local (BOC) and long distance (AT&T) bills in the same envelope.

Defining Functional Divestiture

On passing the three-quarter mark in the divestiture marathon, a pall of apprehension became ever more pervasive as to whether the Bell System could possibly have its operations act together by year's end. This explained the eager agreement to simulate divestiture beginning October 1, thus providing a 90-day shakedown period rather than enduring the chaos—and the risks—of an abrupt transformation on New Year's Eve.

It should be emphasized that the *idea* of simulation—"Functional Divestiture" in Bell System vernacular—was not a sudden brainstorm of mid-1983. Actually, the concept of a test run had been written into the Plan of Reorganization months earlier and was now brought to the fore by the imminence and magnitude of the implementation task. The POR said:

> Personnel assignments will also be completed by September 1983. This will allow the System to conduct business during the last quarter in a "divested mode," meaning that the System will operate its network in a management reporting structure that simulates the operations of the independent companies. Such a period is essential for assuring uninterrupted service when AT&T in fact divests the BOCs on January 1, 1984.

In retrospect, the passage was remarkably creative, if not downright prescient. In fact, no one knew precisely what "divested mode" really meant at the time it was written. It was not until the third quarter of divestiture's second year that the scope and difficulty of the job were fully realized. (Not inappropriatedly, splitting 200 million customer records three ways among the regionals, AT&T Information Systems, and AT&T Communications was one administrative function often cited to illustrate the extent of the task. Nonetheless, it still did not approach in intricacy the chore of tearing apart vast computer systems.)

Functional divestiture was clearly a step in the right direction. However, it introduced its own complexities as well. For example, a dress rehearsal would require a complex matrix of reporting relationships between old and new organizations, and some extraordinary procedures for dealing with customers who knew full well the Bell System would not be split apart until the New Year. "Why," they would certainly ask, "do I have to deal with three companies even before divestiture?" It would be a difficult question to answer to their satisfaction.

The definition and direction of functional divestiture fell to Larry Mead, who was charged with overseeing implementation of the operations aspects of divestiture. In characteristic fashion, Mead developed an effective and highly detailed road map for the Bell System to follow in getting to October 1. His plan, bound in a bright yellow cover and entitled *Profile of Operations,* soon became the guide for divestiture planners throughout the Bell System. It defined more than 100 operational attributes—a truly imposing number—that would have to be in place to achieve divestiture. ("Attributes" were significant changes to be made in organizational responsibilities, systems, interfaces, etc.) Further, it delineated a "penetration level" for each attribute, suggesting how far into the changeover the company would have to proceed to assure a smooth transition.

The *Profile of Operations* covered seven major areas: provision of customer service, engineering plant additions, maintenance of existing plant and equipment, procurement, billing, contract administration, and organizational restructuring. It was a master—and masterful—checklist for use by a broad array of responsible managers throughout the nation.

Divestiture had reached that point, as one popular commercial had it, where "the rubber meets the road." On July 25, an *AT&T Management Report* article appeared under the headline: "Divestiture Implementation to Enter Crucial Phase." The article emphasized that "implementation is tougher than planning," and that "all activities would accelerate toward year's end." To those of us immersed in the effort, these words seemed a remarkable exercise in understatement.

Disappointment

As the hot summer weeks of 1983 flew by, the Operational Tracking Center indicated that there were serious time problems. Despite the early and unified commitment at the May presidents' conference, the clear road map drawn by Larry Mead, and the continuous meetings and exhortations of AT&T staff units, functional divestiture simply was not happening as expeditiously as hoped.

It appeared that while everyone agreed on the need, the concept, and the plan, a kind of generalized procrastination was forming that would push ahead of itself, like a wave, many of the critical changeover tasks. Penetration levels were not being achieved. And three of eleven key operational areas were reported still in condition "red"— that is, in a state that jeopardized the divestiture schedule: access service implementation, intercompany contract resolution, and business office realignment.

These delays were not born of indifference or failure to accept the very real importance of functional divestiture. They grew out of the extreme difficulties of the tasks, combined with a concern for the expense involved in executing the operational split before D-Day.

Strike!

In early August, adding complications, a nationwide strike was declared against the Bell System by 675,000 employees in three unions. In the best of times, strikes are disruptive, and these were hardly the best of times. A mood of dismay settled over those struggling to make divestiture happen. Management people, many already working the divestiture quarry, would have to fill the void left by strikers in customer contact positions. And needless to say, there was no slack in an already taut schedule. Additional delays would very likely push the effective date beyond 1/1/84 or cause even greater disruptions in the nation's telephone service, especially if legal and financial divestiture were concluded on time while operational divestiture remained unmet.

Nonetheless, a resolute AT&T management made it clear that no slippage of the divestiture date would be considered. Ways to make up any lost time would be vigorously sought; resources that were needed would be made available. Somehow, most divestiture work went forward, often pressing into service cadre staffs left behind as the rear guard.

The prevailing wisdom was that the strike would last but a few days and lost time would be recouped one way or another. But as the first week melted into the second, and the second approached a third, the nervousness among staff at all levels increased geometrically. Not surprisingly, there were curbside suggestions that the union strategy was to exploit the divestiture schedule in pressing AT&T to meet demands. However, there were never any overt signs of such motives. Had there been, it is unlikely they would have prevailed against management's determination with regard to the January 1 date.

Happily, the 15-day work stoppage finally ended on August 21. All hands returned to their jobs, and the pace of functional divestiture quickened again. Still, as October 1 drew near, it was clear that full functional divestiture was lagging. A sense of the aggregate feelings in those tense days can be read in excerpts from a status report that I drafted and submitted to senior management late in September:

It is no secret we are entering a critical phase of divestiture. . . .

Now with October staring us in the face we find we will not meet all the October 1st dates in the Yellow Booklet. . . .

Why are we behind?

1. Magnitude of the job at the lowest level of detail . . . records conversion . . . software . . . gaining agreement on contract matters.

> 2. Changes in FCC Access Order. I have no doubt that if we had all Access Service filings nailed down last April . . . we would be better off today.
>
> 3. In some companies, slight delays because of work stoppage.
>
> Will we make Jan. 1st? We may not know for sure until then. . . .

In the Interim: At Judge Greene's Court

While the intensive internal effort was being pressed inside the business, actions on other fronts also helped to shape the future of both the business and the industry.

On July 8, for example, having approved the Consent Decree (with modifications) almost a year earlier, Judge Greene approved the Plan of Organization submitted the previous December, but not before he had thoroughly considered the sentiments of more than 100 intervenors. Not unexpectedly, the court drafted several modifications of the POR. In fact, the 195-page opinion, replete with 300 footnotes, included a spectrum of changes ranging from pension portability and future liability for past antitrust cases to equal-access definitions and approval of local exchange area boundaries.

Most significantly, the judge assigned the Bell name and logo to the divested companies, prohibiting AT&T from using it except in Bell Labs' nomenclature. Legal and marketing considerations aside, it seemed to me an injustice to deny the parent company the right to preserve its century-old identity, deriving from the inventor of its original product. But to the BOCs, the judgment seemed eminently fair. "One man's justice is another's injustice," Emerson wrote, 142 years before the Consent Decree was signed. Like life itself, divestiture seemed full of ironies and inequities.

Acceptance, albeit grudging, of Judge Greene's modifications by AT&T and the Justice Department finally came on August 3. A special report on the announcement was issued under the headline: "Acceptance of POR Modifications Signals End of an Institution, New Era in Telecommunications." AT&T spokesman Pic Wagner said the approval "has cleared the decks for us to advance briskly into the competitive telecommunications marketplace."

On the FCC Front

But sailing into a truly competitive environment would require one more major move by the FCC: a decision regarding access charges.

Essentially, the introduction of competition into the telecommunications industry had the effect of driving prices toward cost, making it impossible to continue the system of internal subsidies. Consequently, new guidelines had to be adopted for the recovery of access costs. These new guidelines were spelled out in the FCC's Access Charge Plan.

Basically, the FCC plan would substantially reduce subsidies for local service by interstate long-distance callers and require the operating companies to collect fees from both customers and interexchange carriers to cover the actual cost of access. Customers would pay access charges to the companies in the form of flat monthly fees to cover the cost incurred by the companies in providing the connection between the customer and the local telephone office. Residence customers would pay $2 per month per line in 1984, $3 in 1985, and up to $4 in 1986. The business rate during the same 3-year period would be up to $6 per line per month, depending on decisions in the state.

The plan also provided that all carriers would pay usage-based, access-line costs not recovered directly from customers. Interexchange carriers also would pay access charges in the form of usage-based fees for their connection to local telephone facilities as they had in 1983, although new formulas would be used to determine the carriers' charges. Taken together, these charges would effect the desired shift to cost-based pricing.

There were few surprises for AT&T or the operating companies when the FCC spelled out the plan in late August. Nevertheless, the 94-page opinion was eagerly received, especially in that it afforded staff planners another measure of certainty as they devised their tariffs and billing systems.

From a competitive viewpoint, the plan was welcomed as well. The reason, of course, was that to the extent fixed costs could be recovered from the customer, AT&T would be able to reduce its long-distance prices—bringing them more in line with pricing of other carriers, such as MCI and GTE Sprint. Thus, the FCC's Access Charge Plan was a welcome stimulus for a company eager to prove itself in the evolving competitive arena.

By this point in the divestiture drama, the concept of competitiveness colored virtually all substantive decision making. Customer satisfaction had been proclaimed by the board chairman as the overarching goal of AT&T in its drive to the future.

One factor in achieving customer satisfaction would be a new bias toward action, a faster and crisper decision process. As if in demonstration of this principle, three members of AT&T's corporate identity committee and two consultants met in New York on the evening of July 31. As reported in *New York* magazine of August 26, 1983,

> The meeting stretched through dinner and the evening, and at nine the next morning the group converged on the office of AT&T Chairman Charles Brown. They had a recommendation. At 10:15 they emerged with a decision: to keep the AT&T name, calling the subsidiary not American Bell, but AT&T Information Systems. AT&T probably moved faster than any other major name switcher in corporate history.

The Strains of Change

As the pressure of implementation mounted, the strains between divestor and divestee mounted proportionately. Tempers grew short; charges and countercharges were exchanged; blame became a commodity in abundant supply. One memorandum from AT&T to a BOC captured at one and the same time a sense of the deteriorating relationships and of the necessity for continued cooperation in the pursuit of a common goal.

> While it is our opinion that your approach will create substantial opportunities for errors, we and BTL will (nonetheless) assist in the implementation of your proposal. *We cannot, however, meekly accept the acrimonious tone of your letter without some attempt to set the record straight.* [Italics added.]

While such language may seem mild when set against the mores of many corporations in the 1980s, it was not cut out of the historical cloth of the Bell System, particularly in formal communication. In fact, this memo stood out in very considerable contrast to the traditionally courteous and diplomatic culture of the Bell System.

As the final lap of the eight-quarter marathon approached, the educational value of this great corporate drama brought to mind another bit of Emerson's wisdom: "Bad times have a scientific value. These occasions a good learner would not miss."

FOURTH QUARTER, 1983: FINAL RITES

In early October I was asked by Bill Sharwell to prepare a presentation on the status of the divestiture project, to be delivered to the final Bell System Presidents' Conference in early November. As with the Spring Conference, this meeting would be split into two sequential sections: the first 2 days for the top managers of the "new" AT&T; the final 2 days for the combined AT&T-BOC officer body.

It did not require a burst of insight to anticipate that a certain awkwardness would dog the convocations of those last 2 days. Plainly, I would have to walk a fine line between sensitive issues in my presentation, regardless of the substantiveness of the material. For this conference—capping the difficult and sometimes rancorous negotiations of the recent past, and marking the end of many close personal and professional relationships—would provide an emotional mix spiced with nostalgia, regret, and, in some cases, perhaps a touch of resentment.

Further, by November there would be little that senior management could do to influence the course of the far-flung details of divestiture. The particulars at the ends of the business stages were no longer in the hands of the leaders but in the hands of the multitudes, pursuing innumerable activities in their own spheres. The die was cast. The ability to "fix" problems was beyond the power even of the considerable joint authority to be represented at this conference.

Thus, for the purpose of this meeting, it was assumed that divestiture would take place on January 1. Perhaps, it was quietly conceded, customers would be inconvenienced for a transitional period. But calls would go through, bills would be prepared and remitted, and the nation's telephone service would be redefined, albeit with some ragged operational edges.

Given this assumption, what would constitute the most relevant presentation for the presidents' final assembly? After considerable thought, I decided that such a presentation would necessarily comprise two parts. The first would be a complete and final status report on the critical areas of divestiture, with special highlighting of areas in which much more remained to be accomplished by year's end. The second would be a penetrating look beyond year's end to a question that would remain a common point of reference for all postdivestiture entities: How will the customer feel as he moved from his familiar "one-stop shopping" to the complicated telecommunications environment next year? More specifically, how much disruption and confusion was the customer likely to experience?

Preparation of the first segment would not be especially difficult, since tracking systems were still monitoring divestiture tasks on a weekly basis, and authoritative and updated information could be obtained.

However, the second segment was a different problem, requiring a considerably more creative solution. In fact, to answer the questions it posed, a camera crew was dispatched to the Orange County, California, business offices of AT&T and Pacific Telesis, sites that represented the advance guard of the functional divestiture effort. At those offices, actual customer calls were videotaped, thus creating a vivid documentary on what future customers could expect when dealing with Pacific Telesis for provision of the line to the house or office, with AT&T Information Systems (or other vendors) for telephone equipment, and with AT&T Communications (or others) for long-distance service.

The substance of the two-part presentation provides a clear if compact picture of divestiture during its final quarter. And so, excerpts of both parts are recalled in the following section.

Excerpts of Part One: A Perspective on Where We Stand

The title of the presentation was "Divestiture Implementation: A Perspective on Where We Stand." In its introduction, the collective, often extraordinary contributions of all the Bell Companies to the divestiture project were generously recognized. Also, the "sensitivities" noted earlier were addressed at the very beginning:

> We should not use this forum to debate issues that might remain. . . .
>
> Controversy has been inherent in our task. . . .

With respect to the status of each of the eleven major areas tracked throughout divestiture, a color-coded pie chart was used (Figure 5).

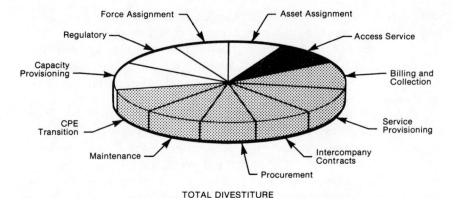

TOTAL DIVESTITURE

FIGURE 5. Divestiture implementation status report—November 1983. (Key: the areas designated as green are clear in this diagram; the shaded wedges are those designated as yellow; the solid black wedge is that designated as red.)

The text noted:

> Asset Assignment, Force Assignment, Regulatory Matters and Capacity Provisioning are in good shape, or "green condition." This is not to say there isn't a lot of work remaining . . . but we expect to overcome any problems.

It continued, somewhat less confidently:

> There is considerable concern about some operational projects—CPE Transition, Maintenance, Procurement, Intercompany Contracts, Service Provisioning, and Billing and Collecting . . . hence they are shown in "yellow condition."

The presentation then proceeded to the issue that would come to rival the plight of the legendary Sisyphus, condemned by the gods to roll a huge stone to the summit of a hill, only to have it fall back to the valley each time, so that the endless and unavailing effort might be renewed:

The only project remaining in serious condition is Access Service. . . . It is shown in red to indicate that while we are encouraged by progress, we are still concerned about our abilities to deal effectively . . . with changes brought about by outside forces (e.g., the FCC, Congress, the State Public Service Commissions).

Overall divestiture is projected as "yellow condition" connoting considerable concern remains in regard to our achieving an adequate divestiture.

These were, of course, potent words this late in the divestiture game. However, there was still much to be done, and the state of the vast transition was such that an unequivocal "all-systems-go" report could not be given.

Excerpts of Part Two: The Customer's Experience

The still-yellow and red conditions of critical divestiture projects were disturbing to the assembled officers. Even more unsettling, however, was the film, which graphically depicted the reality of divestiture's imminent impact on the nation's telephone customers in Bell territories. Entitled *Divestiture as Experienced by the Customer,* it documented several actual customer calls to each of the new organizationally separated, but not yet incorporated, business offices.

In each case, the customer representatives explained to the customer why they could not take his or her full order, tracing with almost heroic patience the complex breakup and the resultant fragmentation of services. Predictably, the customers were extremely frustrated by referrals to other organizations for parts of the service request and confused by the entire discussion of divestiture. (Even at that late date, polls showed that a high percentage of the American public had never heard of the breakup of the Bell System.)

It was a sobering revelation for the officers, all of whom had been imbued for decades with the historic service ethic of their culture. However, their concern was mingled with hope that after the breakup a continuing focus on customer service would ultimately restore any degradation of service and satisfy a confused public. In time, it was hoped the intended benefits of competition would compensate for the loss of the convenience of dealing with one Bell System.

The presentation concluded with these thoughtful words:

Our legacy is pride. . . .

Our future is one of separate commitments to serve. . . .

Divestiture represents a reformation of the industry. . . .

Our employees are just beginning to feel the reality. . . .

Our customer education programs have yet to take effect. . . .

There is much work left to be done.

Other presentations on specific issues were made during these two days, and a part-poignant, part-festive farewell banquet for all officers and their wives rang down the final curtain on a venerable institution—the Bell System Presidents' Conference.

More Action in Washington

Inside AT&T, a new acronym came suddenly into currency. It was MIPP, for Management Income Protection Plan, and it euphemistically described early retirement packages offered to 13,000 AT&T Information Systems and AT&T Communications employees in a move aimed at reducing the work force. The offer was generous, and the response positive. It was only one of an accelerating number of changes in those few weeks, changes both internal and external to the business.

In the latter category, for example, the Washington scene saw action on three fronts: judicial, regulatory, and legislative. In the judicial arena, the Supreme Court issued a one-line order upholding a lower court order approving AT&T's Plan of Reorganization.

Meanwhile, the FCC formally approved the steps necessary to complete the breakup of the Bell System, and on November 23, ordered the detariffing of the customer equipment that would be moved from the Bell companies to AT&T Information Systems. However, the FCC turned down AT&T's earlier request not to postpone the access charge plan. This would not be the last frustrating delay

AT&T would encounter in the process of restructuring pricing schemes to reflect costs more accurately. It should be noted that the ultimate objective of this repricing was the elimination of cross sub sidies, in line with the expressed goal of a competitive telecommunications industry. Thus, the uncertainty and regulatory delay associated with access charges plagued the entire divestiture effort.

Equally discomfitting to AT&T's management were last quarter efforts in Congress to pass a bill that would "legislate" access charges. On November 10, the House approved H.R. 4295, which contained sweeping revisions to the FCC's plan—the plan to which AT&T had already agreed and on the basis of which many of its plans and programs had been developed. It represented the ultimate thwarting of management's labors for 10 years to conform its business to the public's expectations and 2 years of even harder work to implement a divestiture that everyone hoped was in the public's interest.

Comment from many quarters was soon forthcoming. "It's a bad idea," *The Washington Post* of October 17, 1983 asserted. "Eleventh-hour legislation isn't the answer. Congress would be wiser at this point to back off and let the state regulators take a look at the divested system before it decides whether national telephone price controls are going to be necessary." Wrote *Newsweek* on October 12, 1983: "The 11th-hour effort has rallied consumer groups against the FCC, pitted AT&T against its competitors and amounts to what Alfred Kahn, former federal regulator, calls 'a national game of chicken with the world's best telephone system.' " "We think the Bell System should have been left in peace rather than in pieces," *Barron's* commented on November 21, 1983. "That conviction is only strengthened by the witless urge in Congress, by no means yet satisfied, to tinker with the settlement."

In a talk before the National Press Club on December 6, the board chairman's reactions reflected the frustration of AT&T's management. "The outcry in Congress has come on the very verge of divestiture when it appeared we would be able to put into effect the plans that had been studied and agonized over for so long." Chairman Brown added: "We have been saying this for a decade, but all of a sudden the message took root. As a result there is a flurry of twilight legislation that attempts to retain the benefits to the local user of regulated monopoly."

He then said that the bill would jeopardize the future of both AT&T and the Bell System companies and called it "an unmitigated disaster" and "an eleventh-hour attempt to play politics with a complicated economic problem." He further characterized the bill as "pure political snake oil!"

Even as the chairman was delivering this talk, AT&T employees and shareholders by the tens of thousands were opposing the bill in letters to Washington, just as they had a year earlier in encouraging the defeat of H.R. 5158. This outpouring, combined with the jaundiced eye trained from the White House and a broadly opposing press, contributed to the tabling of the bill at year's end.

Meanwhile, in another center of power to the north, nearly 1.6 billion shares of newly created telephone company stock began trading on a when-issued basis on the New York Stock Exchange. They were offered on November 21, and the following day *The Wall Street Journal* would report: "The new telephone company stock hit the ground running—and they never slowed down. . . . Trading in the shares of the new AT&T hit a torrid pace and totaled nearly 8.2 million shares. Volume in stocks of the seven new regional companies added up to 3.2 million shares. Combined, they accounted for 9.7% of the total Big Board composite trading."

AT&T was no longer the ultimate widows'-and-orphans' stock. But the market had become the balloting place where investors could register their relative confidence in the company's competitive future. The activity on Wall Street spoke volumes about that confidence.

As the last days of 1983 ebbed away, external developments incident to the dissolution fell into place. Internally, too, a flurry of last-minute organizational activities was evident. Perhaps the most astonishing of these wrap-ups was the signing of roughly 700 contracts between AT&T and the divested companies, comprising over 1 million pages. One miscalculation of early planning was the underestimation of the scope and magnitude of contractual arrangements necessary to continue operation after divestiture. This was but another symptom of a changing mode. The incredible integration of operations—and of cultures—within the Bell System had not required specification of the kinds of "terms and conditions" prescribed by legally separate organizations.

The Rites of Passage

In late December, hundreds of gatherings marked the passing of the old and the advent of the new. The final Tuesday-night pre-RIB dinner was typical, mingling the sense of accomplishment with the sense of loss, and ending inescapably in a kind of Auld Lang Syne haze from which the parties, would, of course, quickly recover.

The nation's press also tended to look back that last weekend. *The Wall Street Journal, The New York Times, The Washington Post, The Newark Star-Ledger,* and *Business Week* were but a few of the journals filing stories on the closing moments: "Mostly the phone company gave what it promised: good, constantly improving service at reasonable prices," one reported. Another noted, "Successful enterprises embody ideas and ideals that provide purpose and character. [Theodore] Vail gave both, and the effects endured long after his death." A third quoted this writer on the divestiture project: "'Pulling this off was an enormous feat with lots of people with tired backs.'" And a fourth noted: "AT&T headquarters employees are scheduled to find a letter from AT&T Chairman Charles L. Brown on their desks. 'Today,' Mr. Brown writes his co-workers, 'is the first day of the rest of our lives.'"

Chapter 3

Restructuring — "Balkanizing Bell"

"We live in a time of loss of the stable state—a period in which stable views of occupations, organizations and value systems have been eroded," wrote Donald A. Schon in *Beyond the Stable State* (Norton, 1973). This is unarguably true. Yet within the borders of the Bell System, where the organizational structure was so ideally suited to its regulated environment, the erosion had been slower and less obvious than in other quarters. Thus, to most Bell people, the loss of the stable corporate state came with jolting suddenness on January 8, 1982. With pardonable self-interest, they wondered first how the break-up might affect them: their jobs, their careers, their opportunities.

The answers, of course, lay in how the restructuring would unfold. Plainly, a top-to-bottom reshuffling and massive shifts of employees among organizational units were in the offing. However, what forms these adjustments would take and how they would affect employees personally would not be clear for months. Fortunately, the challenge of divestiture would soon sublimate initial reactions of anxiety. Occupational therapy would prove the best prescription for the sense of loss.

MFJ IMPERATIVE

The divestiture agreement required that a major part of each of the twenty-two Bell Operating Companies be spun off from AT&T early in 1984. Characteristically, the MFJ's imperative was as simply stated as it was broad: "Separate from AT&T sufficient facilities, personnel, systems, and rights to technical information to enable them [the BOCs] to perform independently exchange service and exchange access." (Basically, "exchange service" means providing local calling; "exchange access" means making local connections to all companies that provide long-distance service.)

However, while the MFJ failed to specify the form that restructuring would take, it did specify two significant organizational freedoms: freedom to reorganize the divested companies in any way management saw fit, and freedom to form a central services staff for them.

Two Major Decisions

As do most freedoms, the two granted in the MFJ carried with them obligations: first, to decide how the companies would be reconstructed; second, to decide whether a central staff should be established, and if so, how. These decisions came quickly—in February—but not without wide-ranging debate on various organizational alternatives. Camps formed representing the extremes. "Hawks" advocated that each of the twenty-two companies remain whole and independent, set free to survive as divested, with no regrouping into regions and with little or no central services support. "Doves" advocated a least-change scenario wherein the divested companies would hang together with one holding company—a shadow of the former parent, AT&T—and a large central staff to provide services common to all.

Fortunately, deliberations of the responsible presidential study groups resulted in wiser courses: first, a regrouping of the twenty-two companies into seven geographical regions, each with a holding company headquarters unit; second, a central staff tailored to meet the joint needs of the new regions.

It had often been said that the Bell System contained all the necessary attributes of a nation: territory, idiomatic language, history, culture, and government. It was now as if that nation was to be Balkanized into nine different states—the seven regionals, a central staff, and AT&T— each having to form a new government, write a new constitution, and shape a new culture.

This view reflected a healthy regard for differences in characteristics that would be found among the regions. As *Fortune* noted in a January 27, 1983 cover article, "Any notion that the breakup is producing a bunch of cloned companies that will respond to the competitive challenge with Rockette-like similarity is wide of the mark. . . . their history, geography, leadership, growth rate and regulatory environments have already begun to stamp them with unique personalities."

With the acuity of hindsight, it is possible now to understand not only how the nine Balkanized states emerged but also how their emergence was planned and managed. Such a perspective heightens appreciation for Charles de Gaulle's observation: "Regimes do not reform themselves." Indeed they do not. However, the MFJ was the law—a central fact of life that effectively overcame both organizational resistance and inertia. Once in motion, the commitment drew on the traditional ethos of the organization to honor it in the most expeditious fashion.

What's Going on Here?

To most people outside the Bell System, the rearrangement of the pieces has been an impenetrable enigma. "What's going on here?" was an incessant query from press and public alike. Part of the problem was, of course, confusion as to the nature of the Bell System itself. Another was the mystery residing in such terms as exchange service, customer premise equipment, inside wire, exchange access, intra-LATA and inter-LATA calling. Thus, a brief conceptual backdrop might prove useful before proceeding to a more detailed account of restructuring.

A Primer on the Bell System Organization

The predivestiture Bell System can be thought of as an organization whose mission was the design, construction, maintenance, and operation of a huge communications network of switching facilities, cables, wires, microwave radio relays, and satellite systems spanning the nation. At the extremities of the network, in homes and work-

places, are connected 100 million telephones and hundreds of thousands of push-button systems and PBXs, which together comprise
customer premise equipment (CPE).

Since every one of these terminals could not possibly be connected by a single, direct wire to every other one, large electronic
machines are placed strategically throughout the network to switch
calls, just as a police officer directs traffic at a busy intersection. There
are more than 10,000 such machines in neighborhoods around the
nation to direct calls within areas up to 20 miles. This community
calling is termed "local exchange." Calls beyond that range are handled by another higher-order network of lines and switches that connect the neighborhood offices. This network directs calls between
communities, cities, and states, just as local switches direct them
between customers in the same community. (It is linked as well to
the facilities of some 1400 independent telephone companies, so
that all telephone users can have access to the nationwide grid.)

The organizational structure for the design, construction, maintenance, and operation of this network was as simple as it was large.
Bell Laboratories designed the network, Western Electric manufactured most of the parts and installed the switches, and the twenty-
two telephone companies made the wire and cable connections,
installed the telephones, and billed the customers. Long Lines, a division of the parent AT&T, handled all interstate operations.

The system and the organization served the country for more
than a century. But when the political winds of deregulation began
to churn in the 1970s, serious problems swept toward the Bell System. Competitors endeavored to enter the business at both ends of
the network, but not in the middle. More specifically, new entrants
sought to manufacture and sell home and office equipment (CPE)
and also to provide long-distance service, but to avoid the high-cost,
low-revenue domain of the local-exchange business. As noted earlier, Chairman Brown had remarked, "We are surrounded by a fence
with a one-way hole in it. Competitors could come in, but we
couldn't get out into their unregulated markets."

It should be recalled that the objective of universal service and
nationwide access was achieved by a rate structure that subsidized
local service largely from long-distance revenues in an amount esti-
mated by the FCC at $10 billion a year. Local service was a business
no competitor wanted; yet to regulators, legislators, and antitrust lawyers, the local-exchange part of the telephone companies came to be
viewed as a bottleneck hampering their deregulation efforts in the
industry. The reason: long-distance competitors such as MCI and

Southern Pacific (now GTE) had to connect through the telephone companies' high-cost local exchange (the bottleneck) to complete their customers' calls. And since no rivals coveted the local-exchange business, it came to be translated into the new boundaries of "natural monopoly" to be regulated.

The bottleneck concept provided both the focal point and the underpinning of the MFJ. By detaching the more competitive customer premise equipment and interexchange long-distance functions from the domain of the local telephone company and transferring them to AT&T, the remaining area (local-exchange bottleneck) was clearly defined. The corporate separation eliminated cross-subsidies in the traditional form, and regulation of local exchange resumed its course at the state level. In effect, the local-exchange companies would become area networks through which consumers would have to originate calls, and long-distance companies would have to complete calls. The charges for transporting calls through these areas would be termed "access charges"; they became the equivalent of bridge and tunnel toll charges to "islands" of customers for the divested companies. Along with charges to be borne by customers to cover the fixed costs of providing and maintaining the access line from the customer's home or office to the local central office—the so-called local loop—access charges would replace the former subsidies.

The acronym conferred on these local-exchange islands was LATA (Local Access and Transport Area). Each state was made up of one or more LATAs—161 nationwide. As examples, Maine comprised one LATA, New Jersey three, and Texas sixteen. Calling between points within a LATA would be the business of the newly divested companies, although others could enter, with regulatory approval; calling between LATAs would be the business of the new AT&T and other long-distance companies. Local-exchange companies would be barred from providing such service.

In sum, the MFJ aimed to separate the more competitive telecommunications services from the natural-monopoly local exchange.

From an organizational standpoint, what faced the board chairman was no less than nine reorganizations in one, starting immediately with the remodeling of AT&T. In the BOCs the eight CEO designates prepared for a complete reconstruction of their altered segments into integrated regional companies. In each, the future company loomed ahead in the dim mists—perhaps a phoenix rising from the ashes of the divestiture fires. If so, as the myth has it, with a reinvigorated youth and 500 years' longevity. Not a bad trade-off.

REMODELING AT&T

Toppled from its pedestal as the world's largest corporation, shorn of its vast local-exchange operations, and freed to pursue new markets, AT&T faced a strategic and structural transfiguration of sweeping proportions. To its top management the restructuring effort offered a rich mixture of managerial challenges. By most assessments, reorganizing the surviving parent company was the most radical of the transformations. It entailed the separation of $112 billion (of $155 billion) in assets; identifying and absorbing 136,000 employees from other Bell units; redesigning and reprogramming scores of complex administrative systems; preparing millions of pages of documentation in support of 467 new tariff filings; undertaking stock transfer details for some 3 million shareholders; writing and negotiating nineteen major contracts between AT&T and the divested companies; taking title to 26,000 motor vehicles and 650 buildings; and, most difficult of all, dividing the nationwide network eight ways.

These efforts—and they by no means exhaust the range—at least suggest why the planning and implementation of divestiture could require the full-time efforts of 30,000 Bell System people, at its peak.

Stating the Problem

The basic tenet of all organization theory holds that "structure follows strategy." That is, the best structural arrangements are those that best achieve the firm's long-run strategic objectives. Unfortunately, AT&T could not enjoy the luxury of simple classical theory, largely because three complicating factors of major significance affected the grand design.

The first was an abundance of regulatory and legal constraints, particularly restrictions ordained in the FCC's CI-II order. As economic historian Robert W. Garnet wrote in the *AT&T Magazine*, CI-II "was a crucial experiment, one that seemed to embody an emerging consensus on both the direction and dimension of regulation and what role the Bell System would be allowed to play in markets subject to competition." Even before divestiture, it mandated that telephones, office systems, and enhanced services could be marketed and sold only by a fully separate subsidiary. The word "separate" dominated the order: separate officers, separate books of account, separate operations, separate space, separate computer facilities, and so forth. Further, it required that AT&T "*reduce to writing and file any transactions*" (italics added) between the separate subsidiary and any affiliated carrier involving the transfer of anything of value.

The FCC's objective was to foreclose any chance of subsidies to the competitive subsidiary from the regulated side of the business. But structurally it also cut off the normal synergies between the technical, marketing, and operational units of the business—synergies derived from open communications and shared information and experience.

The second major factor affecting structure derived from the MFJ. Whereas the FCC order imposed constraints, the divestiture agreement conferred freedoms: most dramatically, freedom for Western Electric to offer its products in the open market and to enter the computer business. This effective release from the restraints of the 1956 Consent Decree was viewed as a quid pro quo for divestiture, enabling AT&T to maximize the technological and manufacturing prowess of Bell Labs and Western Electric and participate fully in the unfolding information revolution.

The third factor, while least visible, was perhaps the most profound. With the local exchange and 75 percent of its assets gone, the new AT&T was suddenly a very new business in search of a new mission.

Historically, the Bell System was patterned after the U.S. government's local–federal division of responsibilities. Within this context, a patchwork quilt of geographical profit centers (BOCs) served the local communities of the nation, while a large corporate headquarters, acting not unlike the central government, provided common direction and staff support. Given the singleness of mission and similarity of operations among BOCs, all other units in the system could be structured to serve them. These included, in addition to headquarters, a research and development laboratory (Bell Labs) to introduce new technologies, and a manufacture and supply unit, Western Electric, to help fill the supply stream. It was the embodiment of what business scholars today call the "metanoic" organization—coined from ancient Greek roots meaning "large vision." The Bell System was indeed an organization of such vision, and its focus was the operating companies.

This begins to explain the real trauma of the restructuring. For more was lost with divestiture than assets. AT&T had presided over an actual *system* of operations and governance; it was, after all, the Bell *System*. But whereas it could always invoke clearly defined ends that provided virtual doctrinal assurance, a sense of predestined election in its mission, it now faced a crisis of faith. Where it had prevailed by mandate and tradition, it would now submit to the unpredictable, to risk and change. On a number of occasions in its history, the enterprise had been discussed in terms generally reserved for religion. *Time* once spoke of AT&T managers pursuing "an almost priestly calling." And if it is not pressing the analogy too far, one could almost say that divestiture represented for the organization the trial invariably described as "the dark night of the soul," a sense of separation from its secular reason for existence. In addition to those theological considerations, AT&T also faced radical organizational departures. Whereas in the past AT&T's management had presided over similarities among units, it now saw differences between the emerging organizations. With divestiture, AT&T headquarters no longer had operational staffs with counterpart units in the profit centers. Also Western Electric and Bell Labs lost their corporate ties to their major customers, the BOCs.

As if such internal stress was not enough to challenge AT&T's management, the telecommunications marketplace figuratively exploded during 1982 and 1983. Sensing wide-open and nearly unlimited markets, new equipment manufacturers exploited suddenly opened windows of opportunity, even as established common carriers were expanding their own operations to capitalize on the mushrooming competitive environment. For example, Northern Telecom's investment jumped 33 percent between 1981 and 1984. MCI's revenues and investment more than doubled in the same period. And foreign entrants into telecommunications caused the balance of payments in connection with communications to shift more than $200 million in the 1981–1982 time frame. Thus the necessity to respond quickly added further to AT&T's structural challenges.

"It isn't so much that hard times are coming," Groucho Marx once said, "it's mostly that softer times are going."

The Conceptual Framework

Chiefly, AT&T needed a new framework for its organization—in its simplest form, a drastic decentralization and downsizing of the corporate staff and the formation of two large sectors: one to conduct the regulated part of the business, and the other the unregulated part.

More specifically, a small corporate staff would provide broad governance, administration, strategic direction, financial control, and general policy. The two sectors would operate with a high degree of autonomy within the corporate framework, each free to organize in the most effective fashion to meet its market conditions within any limits still prescribed by external regulation.

No deep structural analysis was needed to arrive at this configuration. The huge central staff, geared to supplant otherwise redundant functions in the operating companies, was no longer needed. And the separation of regulated and unregulated operations occurred as a natural consequence of governmental concerns over cross-subsidy. The challenge to AT&T's management was *how* the three structures would be formed, given the enormous shifts in mission, personnel, and function cited earlier.

Unbundling the Corporate Headquarters

AT&T's first task was to reduce its General Departments staff from almost 13,000 to less than 2000. That staff, designed decades earlier to exploit the economies of scale inherent in the commonality of operations among the Bell companies, had doubled and redoubled in size during the 1970s, much to the dismay of those who had to pay the bill, namely the Bell companies. Even top management at AT&T manifested discomfort and frustration at this steady expansion. However, the inexorable growth was not the accumulation of bureaucratic fat; it was an unavoidable response to relentless demands occasioned by the legal, legislative, regulatory siege described throughout this volume. Thus, if one silver lining was to be found in the whole reformation, it would be retrenchment of the corporate staff.

The downsizing effort, euphemistically dubbed "functional realignment," gave many staff members the unsought opportunity to facilitate their own removal from AT&T. I was assigned the dubious privilege of overall planning, coordination, and implementation of the project, and it occurred to me at the time that "central staff redeployment" might have been a more descriptive term for what we were about—although a staff member suggested that "Apocalypse Now" might be even more apt.

The core question in mid-1982 was: How can more than 11,000 central staff employees be redeployed to the emerging organizational units? Already, the corporation was planning the transfer of 2000

General Departments people to American Bell Inc., the separate subsidiary later to be renamed AT&T Information Systems, and the resulting internecine struggles for turf and people were jarringly out of keeping with the traditionally cooperative Bell System culture. Fortunately, despite the larger and more complex nature of the later effort, less heat and more light prevailed.

The methodology used for functional realignment was basically a step-by-step process:

Step 1   *Force freeze declared:*   A no-growth proclamation was issued on April 30 by the top management Budget Review Committee. The purpose: to prevent padding of staffs in anticipation of losses.

Step 2   *"Strawman" structural assumptions developed for prospective postdivestiture organizations:*   These assumptions took on the character of best-guess extrapolations of organizational structure for the new AT&T—no mean task, given the fact that it was entering a new and uncertain world in which its whole way of doing business would change.

Step 3   *Existing departments designated as "senders," prospective departments as "receivers":*   Representatives of sending and receiving departments were identified and made responsible for negotiating transfers of functions and employees. Ironically, the initial responsibility for determining specific needs, within the assumed structure, of the new (receiving) organizations fell to the senders, who were deemed to have the greatest insight into what might be required after divestiture. Receivers could, of course, dispute the senders' estimates. (It would be not unlike a pro football draft in which the colleges decide what the Steelers and Bengals need, with the owners and coaches permitted to negotiate for a better deal when the draft was over.)

The dispersion of personnel from old to new units was infinitely complex. Figure 6 depicts the sending and receiving relationships of but two of twenty-nine organizational units within AT&T's General Departments.

Step 4   *Negotiations initiated:* Beginning in the spring of 1982, senders and receivers entered into intense negotiations that would continue until late in 1983. Indeed, a handful of people were not placed until early 1984. Where agreement could not

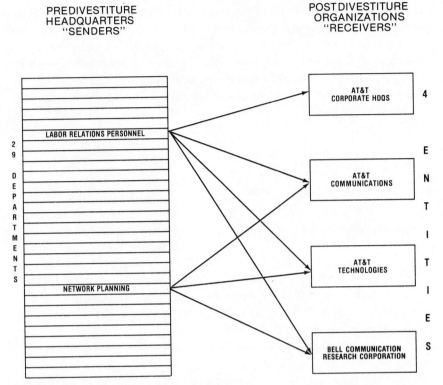

FIGURE 6. Redeploying corporate headquarters—the process. (Predivestiture headquarters are AT&T General Departments.)

be reached, decisions were escalated up the chain of command.

Step 5 *Total plan presented to top management:* The first full plan was presented to the Budget Review Committee on August 24, 1982. Although the force freeze was still in effect, the prospective units reported that owing to new demands created by divestiture, they would be understaffed by 7000 people in early 1984 if relief was not forthcoming. Significantly, approval for growth was not granted, on the basis that new additions would have to be justified through the incipient business planning process.

Step 6 *Plan implementation:* Implementation of the plan began immediately upon approval, according to agreements reached during the intense negotiations during the summer of 1982.

Despite strenuous, sometimes bitter bargaining between senders and receivers, new assignments were virtually complete by mid-1983. To be sure, some staff members felt misplaced—a few even displaced—underscoring the unavoidable pain of restructuring. But in light of its magnitude and unwieldiness, that functional realignment got done at all was one more demonstration of Bell's extraordinarily cooperative culture.

The Final Result

Over the next 16 months, the historic General Departments ebbed away and the new organizations took form. As Figure 7 shows, AT&T Communications absorbed almost half (5800) of the former headquarters staff. Nearly 2000 remained in the new corporate headquarters unit; 2400 were transferred to the BOC central staff now known as Bell Communications Research; 1000 joined the newly formed American Transtech Corporation, the stock and bond administrative subsidiary; and close to 900 moved to a new real estate subsidiary, the Resource Management Company.

SENDING DEPTS.	RECEIVING ENTITIES						
PREDIVESTITURE AT&T CORP. HDQS.	POSTDIVESTITURE AT&T					BCR	TOTAL
	C.H.	COMM.	TECH.	RMC	A.T.		
Executive	40					10	50
External Aff.	370	200		10		40	620
Personnel	280	120	10			30	440
Legal	70	470	100			30	670
Finance	730	520			210	770	2230
Planning	140		50			70	260
Operations		1920	1170			850	3940
Data Systems	90	2110				280	2480
ASD/195	20	520	20	890		290	1740
TOTAL	1740	5860	1350	900	210	2370	12430

FIGURE 7. Redeploying corporate headquarters—final results. (AT&T predivestiture corporate headquarters is composed of the following General Departments: C.H.—Corporate Headquarters; Comm.—Communications, Tech.—Technologies; RMC—Resource Management Corporation; A.T.—American Transtech Corporation; BCR—Bell Communications Research Corporation. The numbers are based on November 1983 data for redeployment effective January 1, 1984.)

As divestiture neared, the last remaining headquarters employees were functioning in their new organizations, ready for the "Bell" to toll at midnight on December 31, 1983. Underlining the poignancy of change, as noted, the grand old building at 195 Broadway was sold in favor of the new headquarters facility at 550 Madison Avenue. Yet the new building had been planned long before the divestiture decision, and the timing of the move might just as well have underscored a decisive break with much of the past. After 195 Broadway had been vacated, scores of people returning for records or personal items remarked on the eerie ambience of the empty building. Like the ghost of Hamlet's father, the presence of past generations of Bell officers and managers seemed almost palpable in the halls. Most visitors shrugged and hurried on to their next meetings, preoccupied as they were with the new challenges that lay before them. Not least among these was the formation of the two powerful sectors, AT&T Communications and AT&T Technologies, which together would supply the heartbeat, muscle, and sinew of the business.

FORMING AT&T COMMUNICATIONS: UNIFICATION WITHIN BREAK-UP

At AT&T Communications' sleek network operational center in Bedminster, New Jersey, stands an enormous, semicircular, 80-by-20-foot control board, its color-coded lights registering the moment-to-moment ebb and flow of America's long-distance calling patterns. It is the industry's equivalent of an airport control tower, skillfully routing telephone traffic over the North American network. In effect, network control is a 24-hour, 365-day balancing act by small teams that constantly monitor the board and initiate shifts in trunking arrangements as needed to assure the most efficient flow of service.

In a way, the center represents the character and achievements of the sector's predecessor organization, the Long Lines Department of the "old" AT&T. Historically, Long Lines had been a close-knit, autonomous division, secure in its stewardship of the interstate network. Now, its strong heritage of autonomy and achievement had both positive and negative connotations for the formation of AT&T Communications (AT&T-C). Postively, it could provide the core around which the new subsidiary could be developed. Less positively, its mature identity could make integration with other units more difficult.

It was recognized at the outset that the creation of AT&T-C should be approached as more than the incorporation and expansion of Long Lines, that it should bring into existence an entirely new company that would merge and integrate all the regulated segments of the new AT&T.

Thus, the labors facing the officers designated to lead the new sector were essentially the reverse of those confronting the other organizations. Whereas most other leaders were involved in the disintegration of their units—that is, the identification of people and functions for transfer elsewhere—AT&T-C had to integrate people and jobs "emigrating" from twenty-two Bell companies and seventeen departments of AT&T headquarters. This consolidation posed many of the problems and issues experienced in large corporate mergers and acquisitions so much in evidence in the early 1980s. Not the least of these problems is "culture clash," the phenomenon of conflicting values and attitudes toward performance of the people of two entities brought together under one corporate roof. Since AT&T-C was a figurative melting pot of newcomers from many different companies, regions, and disciplines, the potential for such clash was heightened.

Moreover, at that moment AT&T Communications had to accommodate itself to three environments: its regulated past, the immediate labyrinthine blend of the regulated and competitive, and a totally competitive future. Some business economists believed that managing a competitive enterprise was so antithetical to managing a regulated enterprise that managing both simultaneously presented the company with an insurmountable quandary. Regulatory management calls for strategies prompted by regulatory considerations as opposed to the marketplace: pricing is based on averaging rather than competitive analysis; longer life cycles of products are called for; standardized, not customized, product offerings are the norm. And these are just a few in a much larger set of incompatibilities between the two modes. Indeed, the basic managerial mindset is different.

In addition, the federal government would not yet allow AT&T-C to compete free of shackling rate restraints. Fully 60 percent of its revenues were expended on charges for access to the new regional companies' local-exchange lines, charges determined by FCC fiat. And despite MCI's and GTE's strategic pricing moves to penetrate the sector's markets, AT&T could not respond by changing its own interexchange rates except through the long, laborious regulatory process. This, too, contributed to what some felt was an impossible task.

Establishing the Needs

Four major capabilities had to be developed in parallel before full operation was possible for AT&T-C in early 1984. Development was led by Morris Tanenbaum, its newly appointed chairman. Tanenbaum, recognized throughout the Bell System for his keen analytic gifts, enjoyed the rare distinction of having held officer-level posts in all major predivestiture segments—Western Electric, Bell Laboratories, an operating company (New Jersey Bell, where he served as president and CEO), and AT&T headquarters. His broad understanding of the operations of the corporation would provide important background for each of the programs at hand.

First, a strategic marketing and sales capability had to be honed. AT&T had brought its long-distance marketing capability a long way since the 1970s, but divestiture catapulted the entire industry forward in terms of competitive intensity. For the first time, in fact, marketing would require full equality with network operations, historically the kingpin of Long Lines. To underline the fact that the discipline had come of age, Executive Vice President Sam Wilcoxon—responsible for marketing—was appointed to report directly to Tanenbaum.

Second, AT&T-C faced the extraordinarily difficult and sensitive necessity of establishing local units to deal with the forty-eight public utility commissions that controlled rates on calling between LATAs within each state. (As noted, inter-LATA calls—previously the domain of the Bell Operating Companies—had been reassigned to AT&T by the MFJ.) AT&T was broadly experienced in dealing with *federal* regulatory matters, but *state* regulation was a new ball game. And among those state commissions and staffs were many who were, to say the least, unhappy about the entire divestiture episode, perceiving that it had been conceived and executed without their participation. In this view, the decree was a unilateral federal preemption of state authority.

The urgency of establishing a state regulatory capability, and the implications of the FCC's access charge deliberations, magnified the significance of AT&T-C's environment to its fortunes. That significance was recognized by the appointment of another executive vice president, Al Partoll, to lead AT&T-C's external affairs activities. Partoll, an attorney, had held the post of vice president of state regulatory matters in the General Departments. He thus brought experience and continuity to the critically important transition.

One especially knotty issue arose over the small but crucial Federal Regulatory Matters Department that had traditionally resided in the General Departments. AT&T-C argued that this organization should be theirs. Interstate revenues were so vital to the sector's economic health, they asserted, that they could hardly be held accountable without that function. However, the "fed reg" leadership contended that both the regulated *and* the competitive sectors—indeed, the entire corporate enterprise—were affected by FCC decisions, and that the department should therefore remain with the new corporate headquarters staff. After considerable debate, the latter course was chosen, with assurances of open links between the department and AT&T Communications, and the proposition that the matter would be reviewed some time after divestiture.

The third capability entailed the absorption of a huge force of almost 48,000 operators from twenty-two Bell companies. This force, brought together in network operations under the leadership of Bob Beck, experienced a sort of divestiture-in-reverse. Before the MFJ, operator units were enclaves within each BOC. Now, the long-distance operators, who handle collect, credit-card, person-to-person, and operator-assisted calls, were under one nationwide organizational umbrella for the first time. And while they felt the wrench of separation, they also evidenced a lift in morale at joining their "kin" from other companies.

The fourth and final capability needing bolstering was finance. In the overall corporate restructuring, AT&T-C would comprise the entire regulated Line of Business (LOB), a significantly autonomous profit center providing more than half the corporation's revenues and, it was hoped, a good share of its net income. This implied a considerably heavier burden than that carried by Long Lines as one of about twenty operating units. To shoulder it successfully, AT&T-C clearly would require outstanding financial competence. Vice President and Chief Financial Officer John Harrington was appointed to head the function, and top-line financial and data processing units from Long Lines and the General Departments were amalgamated under his control.

Putting It All Together

AT&T Communications was now ready to put its new structure into place (see Figure 8). Characteristically, the process proceeded from

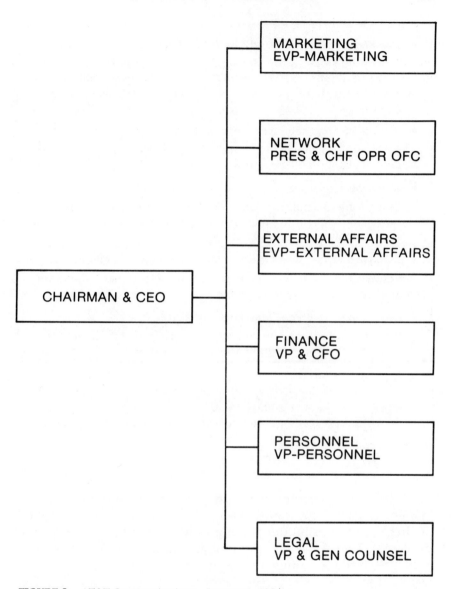

FIGURE 8. AT&T Communications—January 1, 1984.

top to bottom: first, the officer cadre was formed, then each officer assumed responsibility for organizing his unit. The principle members of that cadre, each reporting to Mr. Tanenbaum, were:

- *Bob Kleinert*, President and Chief Operating Officer

  Responsible for AT&T-C's far-flung network operations. These operations would absorb 700 General Departments network staff employees, 48,000 BOC operators, and almost 4000 BOC network employees.

- *Sam Wilcoxon*, Executive Vice President, Marketing

  Responsible for all marketing and sales, to include all costs and pricing, regulatory and competitive.

- *Al Partoll*, Executive Vice President, External Affairs

  Responsible for public relations and business relations with other carriers throughout the telecommunications industry, as well as of all state regulation for AT&T-C.

- *John Harrington*, Vice President and Chief Financial Officer

  Responsible for strategic planning, all financial matters, and development of data processing systems.

- *Bob Gaynor*, Vice President, Personnel

  Responsible for both normal personnel matters and the central mission of "cultural" integration of the diverse units being brought together.

- *Al Green*, Vice President and General Counsel

  Responsible for all legal matters. After active service in the CI-II and divestiture proceedings, Green brought with him a staff of nearly 500 people from the General Departments.

Once the superstructure was in place, the organizational development cascaded downward, with each officer designing and integrating the responsibilities flowing to his or her unit. As might be expected, there was joint planning among departments. However, each was given the latitude to determine its own final structure. Ultimately, four departments (operations, marketing, regulatory, and legal) elected to organize their operations along geographical rather than functional lines. This resulted in noncongruent regions, a consequence that later would cause coordination strains.

In sum, the organizational approach was a conservative one. However, everyone recognized that what resulted was but step 1, a pilot structure. AT&T Communications will change again in the future, although the change will, in all likelihood, be more incremental than radical as it meets its evolving challenges in the marketplace.

RESTRUCTURING AT&T TECHNOLOGIES: A TEXTBOOK CASE IN ORGANIZATIONAL TRADE-OFFS

When he addressed the senior management team of the "new" AT&T for the first time, Chairman Charles Brown pronounced that, "The goal of goals of this corporation is to be the market leader when it comes to understanding consumer requirements and fulfilling consumer expectations." The Consent Decree had freed the company from the "dismal judicial, legislative and regulatory thicket" which had enmeshed it for decades. Now AT&T was entitled under the law to structure and mobilize its considerable research, development, manufacturing, and marketing resources under its unregulated sector, AT&T Technologies.

However, restructuring of the sector presented inordinately provocative, often wrenching organizational decisions. The breakup left it with four diverse subsidiaries: Western Electric, a giant manufacturer ranking twenty-second among Fortune 500 companies, with sales of $12.6 billion in 1982; Bell Laboratories, the world's largest and most prestigious research and development organization; AT&T Information Systems, a new organization chartered to market home and office telephone systems; and AT&T International, an outgrowth of relatively recent Bell forays into the international market.

The thorniest restructuring complexities were rooted in the heritages, the structures, and the orientations of the two older, regulatory-oriented companies, Western Electric and Bell Labs. Western, the company that began as a small model-making shop in Cleveland in 1869 and grew to become the nation's largest manufacturer of telecommunications equipment, had organized to optimize manufacturing efficiency. Bell Labs, whose most precious asset, in the words of its vice president, Arno Penzias, was the "freedom to pursue ideas across the entrenched frontiers of established disciplines," was organized to nourish technological innovation. Neither organization was structured to move its products in the open marketplace. Both had evolved monolithic structures more suitable to single-entity management than to autonomous lines of business targeted to specific segments of the market. Thus, restructuring the two companies into product-based, market-driven business units was likened by some to transforming a battleship and a destroyer into a fleet of hunter-killer subs—and doing it quickly.

The media made much of this problem. Scores of articles questioned AT&T's ability to adapt to—indeed, survive in—the scrambling new competitive industry. One such article in *Fortune* on June 27, 1983, for example, contended, "The world's largest maker of telecommunications gear is poorly adapted to the bracing winds of free enterprise." Of Bell Labs, that same article questioned whether "this transformed institution [would] produce future innovations as revolutionary as the transistor?" More colorfully, *Business Communications Review* columnist Harry Newton observed in March 1982, "No company is better positioned to take advantage of the upcoming 1980's explosion in telecommunications, teleconferencing, office automation and on-line data processing. . . . And no company has a greater ability to blow it in such grand style as Bell."

The challenge was well understood inside AT&T. Organizational ostriches of the past were long since gone. In fact, after more than a half century of stability and success with a structure ideally suited for a steady-state, regulated environment, the company had undertaken two massive reorganizations in the 1970s, essentially to position itself to move forward in an era of gradually increasing competition. In 1973, AT&T and the operating companies moved from the highly efficient functional structure of plant-traffic-commercial to a customer services—operator services—network services structure. In the fall of 1978, the second major reorganization implemented the market-oriented business-residence-network structure in AT&T, and in the operating companies a few months later.

Both edged the corporation toward a more competitive posture. Then the FCC's CI-II order in 1981 introduced even more transforming change by ordering a separate subsidiary for marketing and selling customer equipment.

Of course, most legal and regulatory actions, and most structural rearrangements within the business, had been aimed at AT&T and the BOCs, leaving Western Electric and Bell Labs far less affected. However, divestiture added an entirely new dimension. With the signing of the Consent Decree, the traditional relationships with the BOCs were substantially altered. Western's standard supply contracts with the operating companies were terminated and Bell Labs' research and development efforts would be offered to the companies on a new basis.

The Bell units had also derived greater freedoms: Western Electric, for example, to sell its wares to the world; the BOCs to augment their own procurement capabilities. As *Newsweek* pointed out in mid-January 1982, "The Bell Labs–Western Electric machine, in the past largely restricted to the development of telephone equipment, can now market whatever its deep thinkers can conjure up for the information market." However, in the excitement of their new horizons both BOC's and Western Electric wondered what may have been lost in their forced separation. As 1/1/84 neared, uncertainty hung heavy over each regarding the potential for defection of the other after divestiture.

These uncertainties placed extreme pressure on Western Electric to develop marketing and sales capabilities as quickly as possible, capabilities that would serve both to retain the business of former "vital partners"—the term that had been used for years to describe the relationships between Western Electric, the BOCs, and Bell Labs—and to generate business among prospective new customers. Anticipating this need as early as January 22, 1982, Paul Zwier, executive vice president of Western Electric, candidly told reporters at *The New York Times* "A new market function has to be developed by someone. It could be AT&T or Western Electric. . . . The company will shape itself much more like other large recognized technology companies such as IBM, GTE and RCA."

Establishing the Needs

What had to take place within the Technologies sector was more than a change in organizational structure; it was nothing less than a fundamental change in organizational philosophy. Formerly, for example, decisions on how research and development dollars were allocated were the province of tricompany councils comprising high-level staff executives from AT&T headquarters engineering, Bell Labs development, and Western Electric manufacturing divisions. These councils wielded power and persuasiveness customarily vested only in top officers of other corporations. That is, *they* decided not only what products would be developed but also the timing of their introduction—both key marketing decisions in competitive companies.

(Technological feasibility was usually the decisive factor in the deliberations, since competitive analysis and market "windows" were unnecessary for a company with a franchised market.)

With divestiture these consensus-oriented, tricompany councils would be too slow, too cumbersome, too diffuse to stay abreast of, and responsive to, rapidly changing competitive market opportunities. What was needed, AT&T Technologies quickly perceived, were smaller units—profit centers aimed at specific markets, with simple executive accountability. Each of these units, once formed, would have its work cut out for it. Each would have to develop a strong marketing capability, shorten product development cycles, plan an orderly release of product lines into the future, and create new distribution systems—all within a cost- and time-efficient program that would keep products competitive in a rapidly overheating marketplace.

To restructure along these lines, the Western Electric organizational pyramid would become several smaller pyramids; that is, one functionally organized company (for example, sales, manufacturing, finance) would give way to several quasi-autonomous businesses, each chartered to address specific markets. As noted, this was much more than a rearrangement of blocks on an organization chart. It was a redirection of the most basic and long-standing ground rules as to how the company was managed, decisions were made, products developed and manufactured, and markets served—all to be accomplished in a fashion that best served the company's customers, stockholders, and employees simultaneously.

Putting It All Together

Jim Olson, AT&T's experienced, energetic, and ebullient vice chairman and Technologies sector CEO, immersed himself in the planning and implementation of organizational restructuring. Working with a team of executives from Bell Laboratories and Western Electric and high-level management consultants from outside the company, he personally led AT&T Technologies through the intensive study phase and decision process. As he said at one point in the deliberations: "I've sat through endless hours of intelligent debate on the various alternatives."

The outcome of these vigorous deliberations came early in 1983 with the announcement of the several new lines of business, each substantially an autonomous enterprise within AT&T Technologies, as outlined below:

- *NETWORK SERVICES, E. Wayne Weeks,* President

  Responsible for design, engineering, manufacturing, and marketing of network telecommunications equipment, including a range of switching equipment from small to large and the transmission equipment (lines) required to move voice and data signals between switches and to end users (customers). The vast array of electronic products provided by Network Services include:

  > Electronic switching systems

  > Microwave towers and "dishes" and accompanying electronics

  > New state-of-the-art lightwave systems succeeding microwave and cable technology

  > "Subscriber loop" systems for local exchange companies

  > A broad assortment of cable and wire, from transoceanic cable to house wire

- *TECHNOLOGY SYSTEMS GROUP, Thomas R. Thomsen,* President

  Responsible for three subdivisions: Components and Electronic Systems; Processors; and Government. These were grouped together because of their similarity in terms of technologies, markets, and capital requirements.

- *COMMON COMPONENTS, Phil E. Hogin,* Vice President

  Responsible for design, development and manufacturing of electronic components, those integrated chips much publicized as the prime mover in the worldwide technological revolution. These components would soon prove to be in great demand throughout the new AT&T and to outside industries.

- *PROCESSORS, Jack M. Scanlon,* Vice President

  Later called Computer Systems, this division took on the responsibility for transforming Bell Labs' and Western Electric's know-how into a computer line that could compete successfully in the open market. It was a market already rife with strong, established domestic and foreign firms.

- *GOVERNMENT, Warren G. Corgan,* Vice President

  The government unit, later named Federal Systems Division, was established as a separate division because of the federal government's enormous and diverse need for telecommunications products.

■   *AT&T INTERNATIONAL, Robert E. Sageman,* President

AT&T-I had been a separate subsidiary for several years prior to divestiture. By incorporating AT&T-I, the Technologies division was better able to fulfill its objective of seeking and serving global markets.

All in all, the new structure formed logical and defensible group-ings, given Technologies' needs and objectives. However, this iden-tification of market segments and appointment of leadership was but the initial phase. What lay ahead was the most difficult and perplex-ing organizational problem in all of AT&T's vast restructuring effort: that is, determining what degree of vertical integration should be vested in each new line of business.

Jim Olson posed the problem in its starkest reality. "Fully inte-grating the new LOB's would mean nothing less than disaggregating Bell Laboratories and placing product development and systems engineering within each line of business." The spectre of disman-tling the world's most prestigious industrial laboratory, the conse-quent loss of its worldwide identity, and the further loss of the synergies that attend singular management of technology, was mind-boggling. After all, Bell Labs had been AT&T's crown jewel; its tech-nological history was so rich, as Arno Penzias wrote in *Bell Telephone Magazine* in late 1983, "that many of our achievements—the transis-tor, laser, communications satellite, as well as our 20 thousand pat-ents and numerous awards—are taken for granted, almost like a law of nature." Indeed, it was a research and development treasure, pre-served by the signing of the MFJ.

Nonetheless, the dismantling of Bell Labs was a condition of the first of two options that finally were defined, and it had to be consid-ered seriously. Essentially, this option would redeploy the Bell Labs development organization and reassign resources to the appropriate line of business. Basic research would remain intact to serve the entire corporation.

The second option was the halfway house of matrix management: an organizational arrangement that essentially asks managers to share responsibilities and focus on the end results of the corporation's efforts, on bottom-line financial and service goals as opposed to individual accountability for suborganizational results. Under this option, Bell Labs would stay intact but restructure itself along the same lines as the new lines of business. Then, rather than reporting directly to LOB heads, Bell Labs development heads would report on a dotted-line (indirect) basis to their counterpart LOB president. This would, in effect, give the LOB president decision-making authority with respect to development priorities and budget control. But the management of technology—the critical how-to-do-it task— would remain within the supervision of Bell Laboratories.

The decision was a difficult one. The organization opted for the latter alternative: a "strong-dotted-line" relationship between Bell Labs development efforts and the new LOBs. As Jim Olson explained it: "We concluded that the marginal gains [of option one] would be more than offset by reduced effectiveness of the entire sector. In short, by breaking up Bell Labs, we would lose more than we would gain." He also placed everyone on notice by adding: "If, in time, corporate boundaries [between Bell Labs and AT&T Technologies] get in the way, we will change corporate boundaries." It was a promise designed to encourage cooperation in the absence of direct-line reporting relationships.

Figure 9 depicts the organizational configuration of AT&T Technologies on D-Day (Divestiture Day, 1/1/84). The dotted line between Bell Labs and AT&T Technologies' lines of business shows the indirect reporting relationship described earlier. The double line between AT&T Information Systems, the creature of CI-II, emphasizes the regulatory barriers imposed by that mandate: separate company, separate officers, no sharing of product software, no synergies across the double line.

As the AT&T Technologies restructuring unfolded, it became a virtual textbook case in organizational trade-offs. The sector had to be managed as an integrated entity but was made up of disparate elements. The old and prestigious Bell Labs and the still older, venerable Western Electric had to be recast into new lines of business, with new worlds to conquer. Perhaps most important, and most difficult to resolve, were the new roles and relationships among the players, which would have to be worked out over time.

To help achieve sector integration, Olson drew on resources from within AT&T Technologies and the General Departments staff to form a smaller sector staff composed of experienced planners, administrators, and experts in financial control.

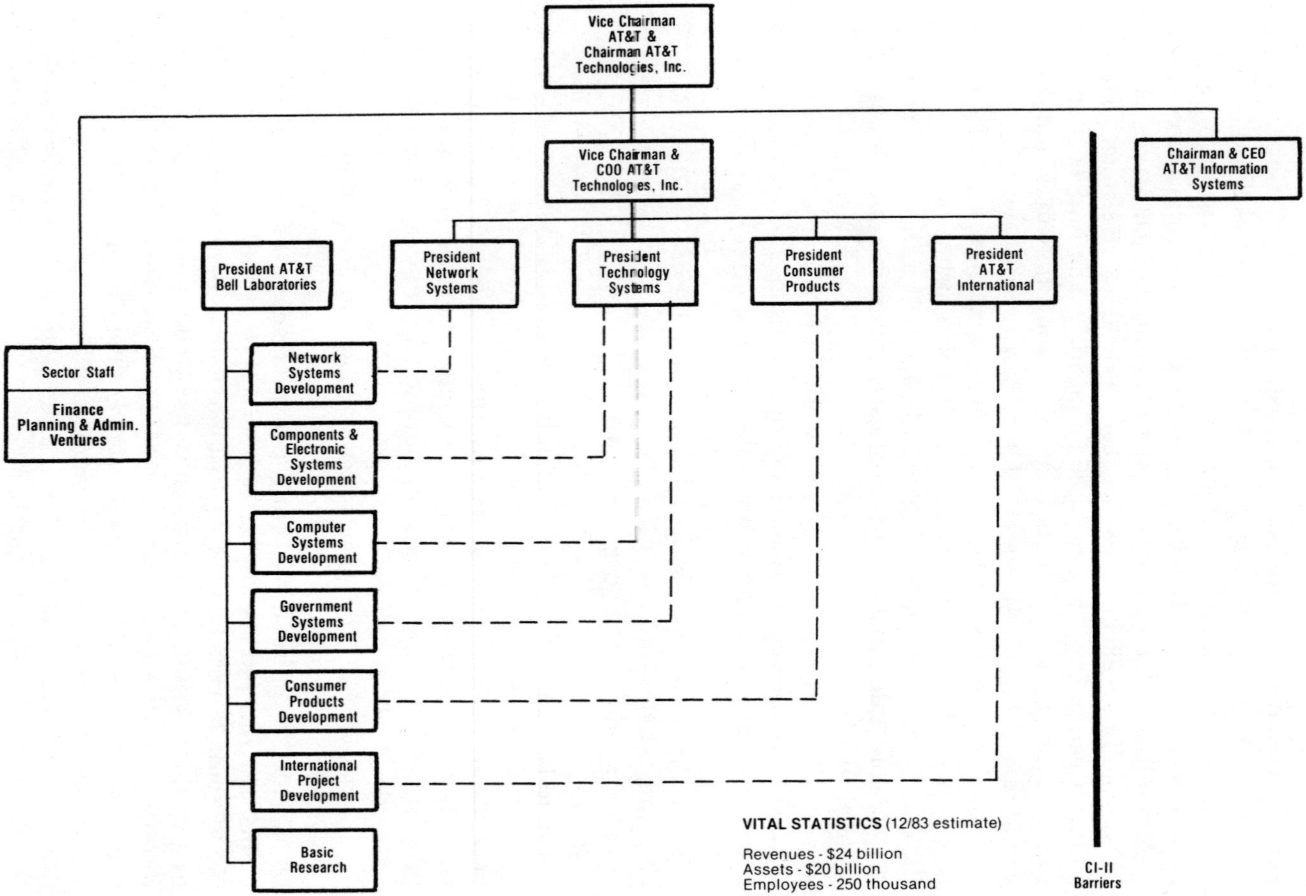

FIGURE 9. AT&T Technologies sector.

The chart contains the following boxes and labels:

- Chairman & CEO AT&T Information Systems
- Vice Chairman AT&T & Chairman AT&T Technologies, Inc.
- Vice Chairman & COO AT&T Technologies, Inc.
- President Network Systems
- President Technology Systems
- President Consumer Products
- President AT&T International
- President AT&T Bell Laboratories
- Sector Staff
  - Finance
  - Planning & Admin.
  - Ventures
- Network Systems Development
- Components & Electronic Systems Development
- Computer Systems Development
- Government Systems Development
- Consumer Products Development
- International Project Development
- Basic Research

CI-II Barriers

VITAL STATISTICS (12/83 estimate)

Revenues - $24 billion
Assets - $20 billion
Employees - 250 thousand

116

Of course, influencing every decision in this immense restructuring was the stark realization that AT&T Technologies would be leaving the starting gates on January 1, 1984, burdened with the high unit costs attendant on the regulatory world. These were not costs of inefficiency: Western Electric had been for decades a model of manufacturing productivity. Rather, these were costs concommitant with providing universal and standardized services; costs, for example, of reliability built into every part of every unit of telephone plant and equipment in the interest of providing superior telephone service over the long pull; costs of maintaining inventories and distribution systems that would provide one-day repair service or replacement of telephones even in the most remote areas.

Now, however, competition was the name of the new game, a game in which the market, rather than regulators or legislators, would determine choices and establish prices. There was much to be done—beginning with drastic cost reductions—if AT&T Technologies was to be competitive with powerful global entities already invading AT&T's markets with lower-cost products.

Technologies was more than ready to compete—indeed, to lead the nation toward what Chairman Brown characterized as "a market society in communications." That readiness, however, was achieved at the price of organizational and cultural transformations of epic proportions.

All that needs to be added regarding the reorganization of AT&T in all its parts is that the job is not entirely finished (Figure 10). Even as this is written there are rumblings that suggest the structure is still settling onto its base; changes of some magnitude may be in store. But whatever they may be, they will unfold more in the nature of sequels to the dramatic story that had its beginnings with divestiture.

REORGANIZING THE DIVESTED COMPANIES

Early Deliberations: The Seven-Region Decision

Restructuring the twenty-two divested companies ranked among the most important and energizing decisions in all of divestiture. The Consent Decree allowed complete freedom for Bell to reorganize the remnant companies as it wished. Thus, the range of alternatives was broad: to leave the twenty-two companies as they were, each an

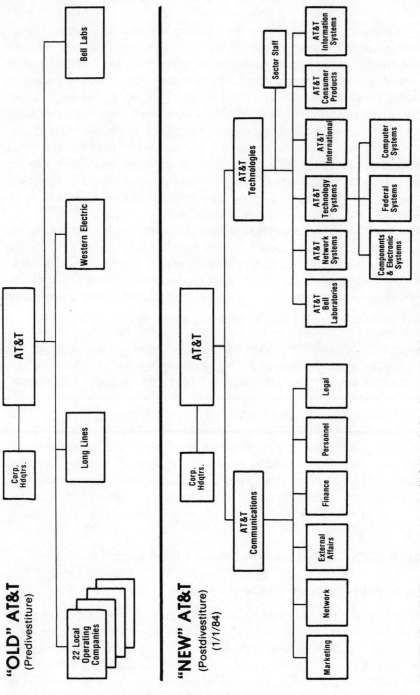

FIGURE 10. AT&T corporate structure before and after divestiture (showing major organizational entities only).

independent entity; to group them into regions; to combine them into one nationwide holding company. There was even a "small is beautiful" party that proposed forty-eight companies, one for each of the continental states.

Ultimately, the responsible presidential study group, comprising five Bell Operating Company presidents and chaired by William Cashel, AT&T vice chairman and chief financial officer, focused on regional alternatives, with the choices narrowing to four, five, six, seven, or eight regions. The group's decision process was guided by a clear mission: "to select a structure which will optimize the ability of the Local Exchange Companies to provide high quality telephone service, earn well, and maintain access to capital markets."

Several specific criteria were formulated:

- No existing Bell Operating Company would be split.
- Regional companies should be of approximately equal size in terms of assets and access lines.
- Each company should be large enough to attract capital.
- Any regional company should have enough states to spread regulatory risk.
- No region should be so large as to recreate the "size and power" antitrust issue that had so plagued the Bell System.

Each alternative was weighed carefully against these criteria, and one by one, those found wanting were eliminated. For example, any option combining four or fewer regions was dropped in deference to the last ("size and power") criterion. At the other extreme, spinning off twenty-two separate companies on their own would not satisfy the "equal size" or "diversity of regulatory risk" criteria. Indeed, it would place the companies' financial credit ratings in jeopardy.

Further elimination proceeded briskly. Potential configurations of companies in five, six, or eight regions did not fulfill the criterion of "approximate equal size." Thus the seven-region alternative turned out to be, by far, the most attractive organizational arrangement. Within this structure, in fact, only two companies posed question marks: first, should New Jersey Bell be grouped with New York Tel and New England Tel or with Bell of Pennsylvania and the Chesapeake & Potomac (C&P) telephone companies? Second, should Ohio Bell be grouped with the Illinois, Indiana, Michigan, and Wisconsin telephone companies, or with Bell of Pennsylvania and C&P?

The solution: New Jersey Bell would go with Bell of Pennsylvania and C&P; Ohio Bell with Illinois, Indiana, Michigan, and Wisconsin.

On February 19, just 6 weeks after the divestiture agreement, Bill Cashel announced AT&T's seven-region planning model. The decision, he remarked, resolved the "fundamental questions from which others flowed." Characterizing the model as the "keystone of planning" for the Bell System's disaggregation, he described how "this resolution will save redundant study and speed the process" of divestiture.

Each of the seven regional holding companies (RHCs) would have its own stock, chief executive officer, and board. And all would start their new lives with significant advantages, to include upward of 3 million shareholders, well-established customer bases, experienced managements, skilled employees, and technologically advanced facilities. In addition, the resources of the companies would be such that if classified as industrials, any one of them would leapfrog at once into the "Fortune 50," for none would begin with less than $16 billion in assets.

For staff planners throughout the Bell System, the seven-region decision was a giant step forward. Now, at least, they had at hand a vision of the organizational makeup of the pieces with which to work. Perhaps as importantly, the decision that was arrived at so logically and promptly provided a rudimentary sense of order in the otherwise chaotic early weeks of divestiture, together with a sense of reality. For many, in fact, the announcement of the planning model was the first occasion on which they believed the breakup would really happen.

Of course, the planning job had just begun. Scores of critical decisions—many involving the disposition of hundreds of millions in resources and strategic directions for years to come—would have to be made within each region. These decisions required the direction and leadership of chief executive officers for the newly announced regional entities. "An institution," Emerson once wrote, "is the lengthened shadow of one man." Now each region awaited the presence of one such individual: to provide strategic direction and administrative control for its fledgling operations.

On May 19, 1982, the names of the seven designated chief executive officers were announced. (Since the new companies would not be incorporated until January 1, 1984, the modifier "designated" would have to be carried on all appointments throughout the divestiture period.)

By any measure, the seven CEO designates were excellent appointments. Each had risen through the ranks, had a strong operational background, had performed as a successful CEO of a predivested company, and enjoyed a reputation as an outstanding leader. It was a case of natural selection among strong contenders.

Curiously, many outsiders wondered how and on what authority the CEO designates had been chosen, whether by the corporate board of directors, the AT&T management, etc., forgetting, perhaps, that the corporation still existed as "one Bell System," with AT&T its owner. Thus AT&T's chief executive officer, Charles L. Brown, was still accountable to all the shareholders and, at the same time, responsible for divesting the companies according to the MFJ, with "sufficient facilities, personnel . . . and *management* . . . to meet equal access requirements." (Italics added.) So it fell to AT&T to decide the appointments as a consequence of its ownership responsibilities and legal obligations.

The stature of each of the CEO designates was itself prima facie evidence of AT&T's resolute commitment to strong management for the divested companies—indeed, to launching the companies with all the resources required to succeed. "Ma Bell will bend over backward to make sure the regional companies are strong and viable from the day they are born," one Kidder, Peabody & Co. authority told *Newsweek* in December, 1982. Even if the "Ma Bell" designation by then seemed a bit archaic, the perception was right on target.

Of course, the regional companies—initially designated by geographic regions (for example, Southeast Region, Northwest Region, etc.)—would require corporate names. This proved an interesting and often quite creative process, the products of which suggested the considerable individuality among the seven new entities. The first to choose a name was U S West, the regional company combining Pacific Northwest, Mountain Bell, and Northwestern Bell. Two characteristics of that choice might have been expected to set some kind of pattern: first, it emphasized the company's regional identity; second, it did not include the word "Bell." However, the individuality among the companies was such that no pattern was to emerge at all.

For example, an acronym—NYNEX—was selected to designate the region formed by the New York (NY) and New England (NE) companies. X stood for "the unknown and exciting future of the burgeoning information market" and the "unlimited quality" of the region's prospects. Bell Atlantic was the name selected for the regional company covering New Jersey and five neighboring states, making it the first of the RHCs to use the Bell trademark in its name. Southwestern Bell Corporation was selected in order to continue the Southwestern Bell Telephone Company's proud nomenclature from the past. The region formed by combining South Central Bell and Southern Bell, and serving nine southern states, was designated BellSouth. The regional company serving the nation's five "heartland" midwestern states, chose Ameritech as its name (for "American Information Technologies"). The last of the seven regional companies to select a postdivestiture name, Pacific Tel, opted for Pacific Telesis Group, explaining that "telesis" is a Greek word meaning "progress that is intelligently planned and directed." The geographic composition of the seven RHCs is shown in Figure 11.

A Turning Point

The appointment of the seven CEOs provided a boost to morale in the Bell Operating Companies. To this observer, it also signaled another subtle yet significant change: the first noticeable breach in the cohesive Bell System culture.

In retrospect, it was only natural. In those early months of divestiture, staff members in the new regional companies were busy taking on a new identity, learning to serve under new leadership, and struggling to discharge the awesome responsibility of "bringing up" the new company. All the while, like the rest of the public, they were buffeted by conflicting accounts in the media, some suggesting that AT&T had cut a deal for itself at the expense of the local companies. It was therefore to be expected that they would begin to move from the collective "we" to a "we–they" philosophy. After all, each RHC soon would be a parent company, too, and the scores of decisions to be made throughout the remaining 19 months could very well affect their corporate fortunes for years to come.

This subtle shift in the culture signaled one of the first real steps in transforming "one Bell System" into a fragmented coalition of nine separate companies, each with its own identity. An almost painful ambivalence prevailed: on a business level, the companies were at the same time customers and ardent competitors; on a personal level, there were feelings of remorse over divestiture itself, mixed with genuine affection for old friends and former colleagues.

These conflicts gained steadily in intensity. That they did not lead to stalemated issues and breakdowns in communication was a

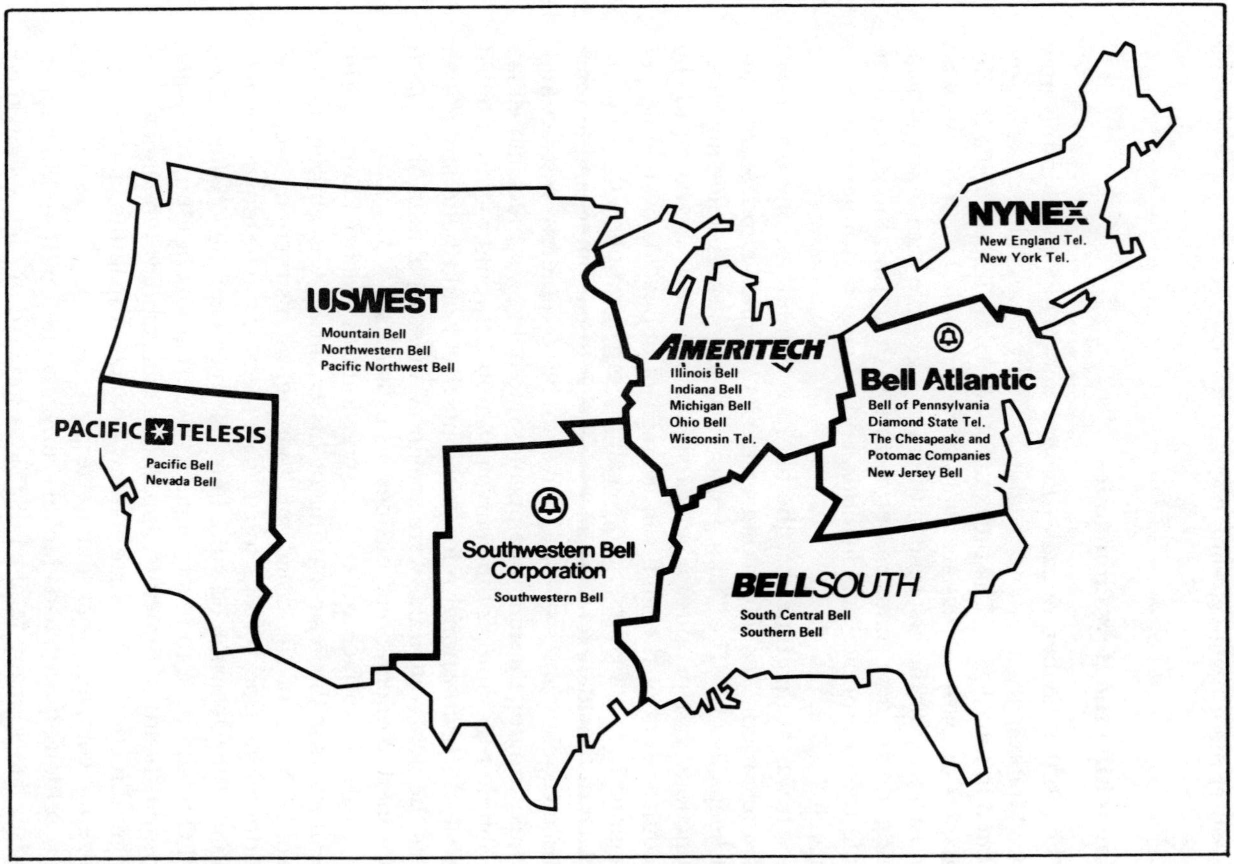
NYNEX
New England Tel.
New York Tel.
USWEST
Mountain Bell
Northwestern Bell
Pacific Northwest Bell
AMERITECH
Illinois Bell
Indiana Bell
Michigan Bell
Ohio Bell
Wisconsin Tel.
Bell Atlantic
Bell of Pennsylvania
Diamond State Tel.
The Chesapeake and
Potomac Companies
New Jersey Bell
PACIFIC TELESIS
Pacific Bell
Nevada Bell
Southwestern Bell
Corporation
Southwestern Bell
BELLSOUTH
South Central Bell
Southern Bell

FIGURE 11. Composition of regional companies at divestiture—January 1, 1984.

tribute to the endurance of the Bell culture, strong enough to weather the ultimate storm.

Launching the New Companies

The job that lay before each CEO was another example in the array of extraordinary challenges laid down by divestiture. As *Fortune* stated in June 1983: "The break-up of American Telephone and Telegraph Company . . . has set off a frantic scramble by executives who must, many for the first time in their lives, grapple with strategic planning, devise new ventures, restructure their organizations, reconstitute their corporate personalities, and come up with new names to match."

It was at this time that the oft-quoted simile of one officer was first recorded: "It's like taking apart a 747 in midair and making sure it keeps flying." The "taking apart" aspect meant identifying those functions and people to be reassigned to AT&T according to the requirements of the MFJ—an average of about 20,000 people per region. Then, of course, the remaining organizations—those left in place to provide exchange access service to customers and to long-distance companies—would have to be completely restructured. Thus, bringing these new companies into being was much more than a simple regrouping of the surviving units. It would require a broad front of organizational reform, reform that would belie any notion that the new companies were somehow an extrapolation of the past, destined to operate on a business-as-usual basis.

Turning to face his new responsibilities, each CEO designate realized that the restructuring of his company was entirely in his hands. None of the usual methodological instructions would be forthcoming from AT&T's top management or the headquarters staff, none of the accustomed guidelines on how to get the job done. Each CEO would have to incorporate his new regional holding company, form its board of directors, appoint its officers, develop its new strategic directions, formulate its new financial capability, and reorganize the company from stem to stern.

Seldom, if ever, had chief executives of multibillion-dollar enterprises had so many seminal decisions to make in such a short time. It was fortunate, indeed, that the Bell System had developed the executive depth to appoint seven CEOs equal to the task. The following sections expand on the elements of that task as viewed from outside the orbit of the RHCs.

Incorporation

The legal act of incorporating was relatively simple, consisting essentially of filing papers within the state to charter the corporation. However, fulfilling regulatory, tax, and other legal obligations was quite another matter. Each RHC was required to register with the Securities and Exchange Commission, the Federal Communications Commission, the states in which they would operate, the New York Stock Exchange, and all the financial institutions with which they would be doing business. (It was drolly observed that the coincident turnaround in the economy during the period was more a result of divestiture-related full employment for lawyers, financial houses, and consultants of every variety than of increased housing starts, deficit spending, and other normal economic measures.)

Over and above these corporate administrative actions, a plan for establishing and maintaining relationships with share owners and other investors had to be devised. As *The Wall Street Journal* noted on October 12, 1982, the organization "raised a thicket of financial, legal and mechanical questions about what investors will receive from AT&T's spinoff of its 22 telephone operating companies." The financial side of the divestiture is only 10 per cent of the overall problem, added an E. F. Hutton first vice president, "and the financial side is mind-boggling."

In addition, there was no precedent for the RHCs "inheriting" 3 million shareholders overnight—3 million who, as Chairman Brown noted, "will become, in effect, 24 million" (eight new companies—seven RHCs plus AT&T—each with 3 million shareholders). The new CEO designates were particularly keen to begin shareholder relationships—as early as a year before divestiture. The corporate problem was that each of the eight entities would be vying for the current shareholders' loyalty and future shareholders' investments. If, during the transition, each competed without coordination, the result could be terribly confusing to investors and to the financial community. After extensive discussions between AT&T and RHC principals, reasoned ground rules for dealing with the financial and investing communities were hammered out—and followed.

The complexities of shareholder-financial challenges to each RHC were but perspectives in microcosm of what the CEO designates had to face during their passage to the new era.

Assuming Ownership Responsibilities

"With ownership goes responsibility," the adage says. And with the prospective passing of ownership of assets from AT&T to the RHCs, a host of new responsibilities, including many performed in the past by the venerable General Departments of AT&T, would be assumed by regional company management.

A partial listing of these responsibilities, gleaned from a much larger inventory, provides another measure of the breadth and depth of the task encountered by each CEO in mid-1982. Separated into four groupings—planning, finance, operations, and external affairs—these are but a sampling of capabilities that had to be in place for the RHCs to operate as integrated units in 18 months' time.

Planning Functions

- Ensuring that transcendent goals (as universal service had been, formerly) are redefined, disseminated to, and understood by all employees
- Developing a regional perspective for planning purposes (for example, environmental assumptions, economic forecasts, etc.)
- Preparing a new regional strategic direction
- Designing and implementing an organizational structure in harmony with strategic objectives

Financial Functions

- Analyzing capital structure, cost of capital, investor attitudes, investment risk
- Managing cash requirements formerly provided by AT&T's pool of funds
- Maintaining and operating a dividend and interest payment and reconciliation system for all classes of stock and debentures

- Seeing to security financing and SEC filings
- Managing institutional investor relations
- Providing actuarial services for financing and designing benefit plans

Operational Functions

- Formulating measurement plans and standards for the quality of customer service
- Formulating network architectural plans for the region
- Formulating policies, objectives, and strategies in connection with planning for growth and modernization of switching, transmission, and distribution plant

External Affairs

- Following legislative and executive branch developments in all areas that affect the regional company
- Developing of public relations programs that establish the new corporate identity (of NYNEX, Pacific Telesis, etc.)
- Interfacing with the FCC and its staff
- Preparing and disseminating annual reports
- Preparing shareholder newsletters for as many as 3 million shareholders

As noted, this is but a small, if representative sampling of the work activities to be assumed by the RHCs. The organizational placement of these functions would vary among the new companies: some to be performed in the RHC headquarters unit, some in subsidiary units, some in the emerging service organization (Bell Communications Research), some even contracted out to vendors. In any case, the responsibility to assure that a capability for each function was in place rested squarely with the CEO designates, even as they created entirely new strategic directions for their companies and delineated the best organizational structures to reach strategic goals.

Designing Strategies and Structures

Alexander Graham Bell once observed: "When one door closes, another opens; but we often look so long and so regretfully upon the closed door that we do not see the one which has been opened for us." The principals in the regions might have recalled this wisdom as they faced up to a strange mixture of loss and gain that formed the backdrop for decision making.

One of the most specific examples of the former was loss of their "embedded base" of telephone equipment located on the customer's premises. (Indeed, people quipped about the possibility of the surviving telephone companies owning no telephones.) The companies also faced the loss of LATA-to-LATA calling within states. And, of course, the loss of direct corporate ties to Bell Laboratories and Western Electric.

The counterbalancing benefits began with the advantage of gaining ownership of assets and the freedom to run their own businesses. For example, the companies would have the freedom to enter into new ventures in telecommunications—and, with court approval, into other areas as well—and to augment their capabilities in the procurement functions hitherto largely supplied by Western Electric. .

By virtue of the court's modification of the MFJ, the regional companies had a flying start on branching out beyond the exchange and exchange access business. Judge Greene had bestowed upon them the Bell name and logo, the lucrative *Yellow Pages Directory* business, and the cellular mobile telephone function. Each had positive strategic overtones.

Nonetheless, each CEO found himself facing a host of long-term strategic decisions on questions that for most companies evolve incrementally over years rather than months:

- What should the business comprise in the next 10 to 15 years?
- What markets and what products should we pursue at the start? Where will we get those products?
- What will our pricing strategies be? What about service strategies, such as custom calling, centrex, service differentiation?
- Should we seek joint ventures? Acquisitions?

Just 6 months earlier, not one of these strategic questions was among the major concerns of the BOCs. Now the answers could determine the prospects of the new companies for years to come.

Perhaps surprisingly, the answers would vary considerably among regions. To understand this is to remember, however, that each had its own rich mixture of BOC and state histories, economic situations, regulatory climates, and degree of operational and technological progress. For example, in mid 1982, the Ameritech region faced severe unemployment in Detroit, while the sunbelt and California companies were experiencing considerable growth. Also, some regions were far ahead of others technologically, especially in electronic switching development—a very real advantage considering their common focus on basic exchange service.

Because of such fundamental differences and, equally important, differences in style and concerns of the seven CEOs, a noticeable divergence not only in the operational context but in the character and culture of the companies began to emerge even before divestiture. In a sense, corporate septuplets with quite different personalities had emerged from infancy and ventured out in surprisingly diverse directions, even though they were bound to abide by the same legal and regulatory ground rules of their governmental guardians. The phenomenon was all the more striking in that each had been born of a substantially homogeneous and integrated Bell System.

Many felt that the differences between regions had always existed but had been constrained by the strength of central direction from AT&T Headquarters. Now unleashed, the differences began to assert themselves. As *Fortune* stated on June 27, 1983, "Although the seven regionals' assets, revenues and customer bases will be roughly the same, their history, geography, leadership, growth rates and political and regulatory environments have already begun to stamp them with unique personalities." Of course, one of the most obvious—and to some observers, the most surprising—manifestations of individuality surfaced when four of the seven regions chose not to use the Bell name in their new holding companies, despite the general belief that "Bell" carried with it considerable market recognition and, thus, value.

All of the regionals would, of course, pursue the same regulated, core business—providing exchange service to end customers and exchange access for long-distance companies to complete their calls to end customers. (This part of the company, under state and FCC regulation, would require structural separation from the unregulated lines of business. As with AT&T, the separation was mandated to assure that no subsidies flowed from regulated to competitive products and services.)

However, on the competitive side, the aggressiveness of the companies was seen in the immediate formation of subsidiaries for customer equipment, *Yellow Pages*, and cellular service. Even more venturesome initiatives were soon forthcoming as well.

For example, Ameritech, the first of the divested companies to offer a cellular mobile radio service, soon thereafter began a venture with Aetna Telecommunications Laboratories to develop a fiber optics technology for the automated office. Southwestern Bell Corporation signed agreements with TIE/Communications and five other manufacturers to supply its newly formed competitive subsidiary with telecommunications equipment that the company would market to business customers. Bell Atlantic agreed to market NEC America Inc.'s newest PBX or telephone switchboard—another step, it said, "in assembling a complete line of high-quality communications equipment to serve business and government customers in 1984."

Predictably, there was as wide a divergence in reporting arrangements as in strategies. Spans of control reporting to the CEO ranged from one in BellSouth to twelve in U S West. Some of the RHCs formed service companies that reported to the holding company managements, others to the BOC subsidiaries. (Southwestern Bell Corporation and Pacific Telesis—both unchanged in geographic responsibility by divestiture—experienced the least change in the postdivestiture mode.)

Figure 12 provides the vital statistics of the regions as of the first day of divestiture.

Company	Assets	Revenues	Employees	Chf. Exec. Off.
	Dollars in Millions			
Ameritech	$16,257.0	$8,344.0	79,000	W.L. Weiss
Bell Atlantic	$16,264.1	$8,323.1	80,000	T.E. Bolger
BellSouth	$20,808.8	$9,799.1	99,100	W.R. Bunn
NYNEX	$17,389.0	$9,825.2	98,200	D.C. Staley
Pacific Telesis	$16,190.8	$8,082.1	82,000	D.E. Guinn
Southwestern Bell	$15,507.4	$7,754.9	74,700	Z.E. Barnes
U S West	$15,053.6	$7,436.8	75,000	J.A. MacAllister

FIGURE 12.   Vital statistics of regional companies at divestiture—January 1, 1984.

In summary, divestiture placed an extraordinary burden on each CEO to develop new missions, goals, strategies, and structures for his enterprise. In confronting the newly appointed with so many managerial challenges, all to be met and resolved in so short a time, divestiture had no precedents and will likely have no successors. But each CEO placed the indelible stamp of his own judgment and style on his company well before the regions went into business on 1/1/84. Beyond that date, the differences would continue to proliferate among the regions—living proof of the impact a leader can have on the character and culture of a company, an influence equal to those of the differing economic, regulatory, and financial environments.

CREATING BELL COMMUNICATIONS RESEARCH: A STUDY IN ROLE REVERSAL AND IDENTITY SEARCH

The Legacy

"My dear, we live in a time of transition," said Adam to Eve as they left Eden. So might the principal managers of AT&T have remarked on change, as they guided the radical transferal of responsibilities from AT&T's historic headquarters unit (General Departments) to the newly conceived Central Services Organization, later to be known as Bell Communications Research or BellCore. To understand the combined travail and excitement of creating the new company, it is useful to understand the legacy from which it sprang.

As noted earlier, the Bell System historically employed the largest central staff in American industry, numbering nearly 16,000 in the final months before divestiture. That staff, supported by a specified contract between AT&T and its operating subsidiaries, traced its origins and its rationale back through the decades to Theodore Vail, the Bell System's legendary organizational architect. Vail defined the General Department (singular in his day) as performing functions "common to all" subsidiaries.

Over the years, economists and managers both within and outside the Bell System would point to the "economies of scale and scope" inherent in Vail's precept, the avoidance of duplicative staff work that would otherwise be necessary for many entities performing the same functions. In fact, no philosophy was more central to the Bell System's concept of standardization (*one* system, *one* policy, *universal* service).

This was the legacy, then: a managerial mindset, especially among the permanent cadre at AT&T, that the best way to do any job was to do it once, at the center.

Apparently, preservation of the benefits of such an arrangement, together with the national security implications of centralization, was of critical importance to the architects of the MFJ. And preserve they did. Paragraph 1, part B, page 3 of the decree states:

> Notwithstanding separation of ownership, the BOCs may support or share the costs of a centralized organization for the provision of engineering, administrative and *other services which can most efficiently be provided on a centralized basis.* The BOCs shall provide, through a centralized organization, a single point of contact for coordination of BOCs to meet the requirements of national security and emergency preparedness. [Italics added.]

The early placement of this provision in the MFJ was interpreted by many as signifying its import. However they are read, two verbs in the passage are of pivotal importance: the BOCs *may* share a centralized organization, and the BOCs *shall* provide a single point of contact for national security. Furthermore, the phrase "services which can most efficiently be provided on a centralized basis" would ultimately have special significance in the selection of functions to be performed by the new Central Services Organization.

When the MFJ was made public, many BOC officers saw no need for a central staff beyond the Justice Department's requirement for a single point of contact with the federal government for national defense and emergency issues. After all, several pointed out, preservation of the central staff was optional; only the central coordination point was mandatory. However, as the BOCs continued planning for the divested environment, the need for a central organization quickly became clear.

The prospect of forming such a central staff inspired the observation that the organization would be unique in corporate America. After all, where else was there a separate corporation of substantial size providing a broad array of technical and administrative services to seven large, Fortune 500, independent companies, each to some extent in competition with the others? Of course, industry associations are commonplace. However, the technical and administrative functions that might be performed by the prospective central service organization, or CSO, are almost always a province within the corporation itself—carefully guarded and not to be entrusted to outsiders.

As a result, many inside the Bell System speculated as to whether such an organization would—or could—be successful for the long haul. If it could, some suggested it might serve as a model for other industries, at one and the same time reducing their collective overhead and increasing the expertise otherwise unavailable within any one company. Perhaps the prototype for a dramatic industrial innovation was at hand, one that could possibly advance the nation's effort to meet the challenge of "Japan, Inc." It was an exhilarating thought.

Role Reversals

The entire divestiture scene was rife with individual and organizational role reversals: subsidiaries became holding companies, clients became competitors, colleagues became antagonists, subordinates became peers, and cooperative followers became rebels. Organizationally, however, it is at least arguable that the most prominent role reversal would be the inversion of the central staff after divestiture.

Prior to divestiture, the AT&T headquarters unit, as owner, carried ultimate authority, the clout concomitant with ownership. With that authority went accountability to shareholders. AT&T was, therefore, directive on matters of policy, finance, strategy, and systemwide programs. It was often quipped that "AT&T, like the Vatican, issues encyclicals for consumption elsewhere." However, its role was the embodiment and the mechanism of Vail's precept of standardization.

Now, in deciding whether to form a central staff suitable to the divested BOCs—and if so, how—it was recognized that the organization would in no way become a duplicate of the General Departments; that in fact, it would experience a 180° turnaround in its role. It would not send directives to companies it owned; rather, it would *receive* directives from its seven new owners, the regional companies. It was as if the needle of the compass of authority was swinging suddenly from magnetic north to magnetic south. Hyperbolically, master would become servant, servant master. This new mode would take some getting used to, constituting as it did yet another culture shock consequent to restructuring.

Deciding to Be or Not to Be

More than any other constellation of judgments in the panorama of divestiture, the decisions surrounding the creation, size, structure, and method of operating the CSO fell solely to the managements of the seven regional companies. After 1/1/84 the divested companies would own and direct the organization and thus bear the consequences of the determinations *they* now had before them. Thus, it was only appropriate that they make the final settlements collectively and without intervention from AT&T.

A presidential study group was assigned to this task, to be chaired by Tom Bolger, AT&T executive vice president. Members included Guinn (Pacific), Allen (C&P), Barnes (Southwestern) and Van Sinderen (Southern New England). Appropriately, this committee became an entirely BOC cadre when Bolger was appointed CEO designate of Bell Atlantic in May 1982.

In its very first meeting, the study group—by unanimous vote—made the crucial decision to form a substantial central staff (in their words, a Central Services Organization) that would provide a capability far beyond the national security requirement in the MFJ. They agreed that such a staff would be assigned the mission of providing expert support to the regional telephone companies, focusing primarily on the technical aspects of exchange telecommunications services and other services that could be efficiently centralized. In contrast to the unanimity of this first vote, however, debate and decision making with respect to size, scope, content, structure, and operation would be prolonged and, at times, painful throughout the divestiture period.

From its outset, the CSO had detractors, chief among them the National Association of Regulatory Utility Commissioners, which stringently questioned the need for such an organization. In addition, some FCC commissioners expressed concern over the potential for the CSO's evaluative work resulting in the de facto promotion of Western Electric products. And several competitors asked Judge Greene to limit the activities of the CSO in his final decision on the Plan of Reorganization.

Nonetheless, the technology of telecommunications shaped the conclusion of the presidential study group that a central support organization would be absolutely essential to the provision of high-quality telephone service at affordable rates in the future. As its president would later comment in an *AT&T Management Report:* "The technology is changing so rapidly that we need a centralized group to stay abreast of it and apply that technology to our business. Much of the talent needed to do that is not available outside the Bell System. You couldn't clone it seven times. And even if you could, it would cost seven times more."

Getting Started

Once the decision to form the CSO was made, Bolger's study group began to give shape and direction to the effort. Early discussions grappled with questions of form as well as philosophy. For example, in a mid-March 1982 meeting that I attended, the six presidents wrestled with the problem of how far to go in the development of the organization. They were, after all, at liberty to create whatever functions they felt were needed after divestiture, yet they would have to exercise care not to replicate the huge General Departments. Several quotes from that meeting reflect the breadth of their concerns:

> Merely moving the General Departments intact over to form a service corporation would only serve to continue "business as usual."
>
> Should considerations of the efficiency of central development outweigh the dangers inherent in size?
>
> If systems engineering is separated from Bell Labs and no longer interactive with research and development, will it "wither" in the central staff?

To explore these and many other such questions, and to develop a prototype organization complete with detailed, functional descriptions, a task force of operating company officers was appointed by the presidential study group. Bill Burns, executive vice president and chief operating officer of New York Telephone, was named to head the group on a full-time, special-assignment basis. Burns's background as vice president and treasurer of AT&T and as a BOC operating executive provided the credibility and stature needed to lead the charge. Other members came from the C&P, Southern New England, Pacific, Southwestern, and Indiana Bell telephone companies. To provide staff support, a small AT&T cadre was formed as well.

Initial efforts began with the consensus that a "leading edge" central resource of substantial size would be required, a resource that would be heavily technical in nature. Now the job was to build that resource, at least conceptually, one piece at a time.

Phase 1: Designing Bell Communications Research

First, Burns's group and supporting staff undertook the incredible task of examining every job and function performed for the BOCs by the General Departments, Bell Labs, and Western Electric to determine which should be continued and which, of those, should be done centrally. Using 1982 budget activity records and project descriptions, each of the hundreds of functions was considered in detail with regard to future needs. Of course, the task force members consulted their own subject-matter specialists for judgments as to whether individual tasks could be performed most efficiently and economically at the BOC level, the regional level, or the central level. Thus a broad network of people ultimately became involved in a vast sorting job likened by some to "cleaning out the world's largest attic."

The functions were sorted out in several ways:

1. Is it local exchange, interexchange, or both?
2. If local exchange, should it be performed by the companies or central staff?
3. If by central staff, is it mandatory? Highly desirable? Desirable? Marginal? Not required?

This analysis continued until mid-June, punctuated by reviews by the presidential study group. In the third week of June, Tom Bolger announced preliminary recommendations by the task force on the overall function and corporate structure of the CSO. This "first out" report, presented for approval to the regional CEO designates in mid-July, recommended a staff of 2324 technical people and 735 nontechnical employees, for a total cadre of 3059. Bolger noted: "These first-phase recommendations will serve as a starting point for work with the regional executives on the precise responsibilities and structure of the central staff." He added that, "As a result of the first phase, the study group has recommended that the central staff be established as a corporation owned in equal proportions by the seven regional holding companies. Its board of directors would consist of the chief executive officers of the regional companies and top officers of the central staff."

On July 14, the task force recommendations were presented to the regional CEO designates, who approved them and agreed to proceed promptly with implementation. (One resident philosopher commented that July 14—Bastille Day, marking French independence—was especially appropriate, since the CSO model provided observable evidence of the imminent independence of the divested companies from AT&T.) Significantly, the CEOs recognized that a number of additional centralized activities would have to be studied during the implementation stage. To spearhead this new effort, the CEOs called upon their recently appointed regional planning officers as a group to replace the ad hoc task force that had so ably filled the breach in the early deliberations and study.

Thus ended the first stage. Looking forward to the next push, Bolger declared: "The second phase of planning will focus on the structure. . . . A primary consideration in this phase will be the planning for mutually compatible regional and central staff operations." This crisp declaration reflected only a glimmer of the considerable effort that still lay ahead.

Phase 2: Implementing the Plan

The Bastille Day recommendations were the starting point for the regional planning officers' efforts in phase 2. And indeed, "starting point" it proved to be. Few realized during those hot July days that the sanctioned complement of 3000 CSO employees would almost triple by the January 1, 1984 changeover date.

Significantly, that expansion would stem essentially from a thorough reexamination of all the tasks and functions explored in the earlier study as new needs continued to crop up, needs requiring skilled staffing to maximize the MFJ's concession regarding "services which can most efficiently be provided on a central basis."

This was especially true of technical services, historically provided on a centralized basis at Bell Labs and Western Electric, and virtually unable to be duplicated. Appropriately, then, the regional planners began to add substantially to the initially recommended core.

As it shaped up, the new company promised to be, as one writer described it, an "interesting new hybrid grafting together offshoots of Bell Laboratories, Western Electric, and AT&T's General Departments." These offshoots were gathered together in a painstaking process relating entirely to future BOC needs.

The regional representatives began by examining ways to assure the continuing development and maintenance of scores of centrally developed operational and administrative systems. Aptly named Business Information Systems, these integrated systems provided for such critical functions as service order entry, circuit provisioning, directory information, and engineering support. Over the previous 15 years, literally billions of dollars had been invested in their design, development, and continued maintenance. To allow this central capability to wither and die with divestiture would be to forgo an opportunity specifically provided for in the Consent Decree and, moreover, to risk unnecessarily the technical efficiency and the quality of the nation's telephone service. Accordingly, by October 1982, the regional planners had recommended that 3281 information systems experts be added to the staff—more than doubling the original complement.

Subsequently, other "pockets" of capabilities were added, all aimed at strengthening the service capability of the CSO. Examples include a document distribution group in Indianapolis and a training center in Lisle, Illinois, near Chicago.

In late 1982, the CSO was given a great deal of added impetus with the appointment of Rocco Marano as its CEO designate. The highly respected president of New Jersey Bell, Marano was the ideal choice not only by temperament and background but also because he was selected from the BOC rather than the AT&T side of divestiture—an increasingly important attribute as the breach continued to widen.

Immediately recognizing the scope and depth of the technical and administrative task of making the CSO a reality, Marano appointed two experienced officers to serve with him: Irwin Dorros, executive vice president, to head the technical staff development effort, and Kenneth Looloian, vice president, finance and administration, to lead the administrative endeavor.

In the next several months, each worked to develop his respective organization's structure, functional descriptions and force numbers, each of which were detailed in two final planning tomes, the so-called White Books.

In mid-March, the regional CEO designates reviewed and approved the general staff levels proposed: some 5200 technical staff members under Dorros, and the remaining cadre of more than 3000 to comprise Looloian's administrative and support services organization.

Fully half of the Dorros work force would be involved in information systems already in use or projected for use at the operating companies. Such computer-based systems include inventory, billing, and record-keeping software—systems like the Trunks Integrated Record Keeping System (TIRKS). Software and systems specialists in his information systems division would handle the burgeoning information systems needs of the regions.

The other half of the Dorros organization would focus on providing research, systems engineering, network planning, quality assurance, and operating methods to support the application of technology in the local operating companies—particularly in local switching systems, local distribution systems, operator service systems, and interoffice transmission systems.

Looloian's force would be responsible for eight varied disciplines, some internal—that is, supportive of the CSO itself—and others external, in support of the BOCs. These disciplines include access tariffs (regulatory matters), personnel, finance, industry relations (with independent telephone companies), public and employee information, comptrollers and information systems, administrative services, and support services.

Early on, the seven CEO designates also established the Principles of Ownership Agreement, which determined the two ways work within the CSO would be funded, in the interest of giving the regional companies maximum individual choice. The first method, called individual funding, would apply to those projects that some regions wanted undertaken while others did not. Such projects would have to be approved by a 4 to 3 vote to ensure that the CSO's resources were being used efficiently, and that costs would be covered equally by the number of regions that wanted to participate in the projects. The second is called core funding and would cover those projects in which the benefits would accrue equally to all regions—research, for example, and matters involving national security. These would have to be approved by a 5 to 2 vote, and all regions would pay equally. "The important thing here," Marano said, "is that all the control is in the hands of the regions. They decide what's going to be done, when it's going to be done, and how much they will spend."

Fine tuning the phase 2 effort continued through the year, and as divestiture neared, support for the CSO among the regions grew steadily. "Reasonable," "desirable," and "necessary to ensure high-quality exchange service" were the ways the companies character-ized the organization's proposed size and responsibilities. They emphasized that the benefits and cost savings to be derived from cen-tralizing systems engineering and technical support functions would significantly benefit the regions, the operating companies, and, indi-rectly, the ratepayers. Surveying ahead, Marano said in an *AT&T Man-agement Report* of March 4, 1983:

> At this juncture, let me say that our attitude in the CSO is to keep what is truly useful and valuable from the Bell System, adapt what seems to need change for our new circumstances, and adopt new paths and meth-ods that seem to hold promise. We refuse to be bound by the past. But by the same token, we refuse to reject everything that is part of our heritage.

Marano's vision was clear and concise and served as a firm tem-plate for implementation. By articulating its mission, by describing its functions and its anticipated values, by setting forth the ways in which the CSO would be funded, managed, and directed, Marano provided the identity which had been so much in question at the corporation's inception. However, as he pointed out, it was still to be, at least for a time, a corporation in search of its own name:

> To call the new entity the Central Services Organization is something like describing your spouse as the co-tenant of your home. It's accurate as far as it goes, but it sure doesn't begin to describe what the relation-ship is all about. So we're in the process of coming up with a name.

Some weeks later, the new name—Bell Communications Research—was announced. It seemed especially appropriate, not only because of the essential technical research and development functions it would provide but also because of the nature of the peo-ple it would bring together. (As noted in the same *AT&T Manage-ment Report*, "Over two-thirds are going to be telecommunications specialists of proven skills and ability. About half of these will come from Bell Labs. . . . We also will be getting some of the best and brightest engineering, research, and systems people from Western Electric and AT&T.")

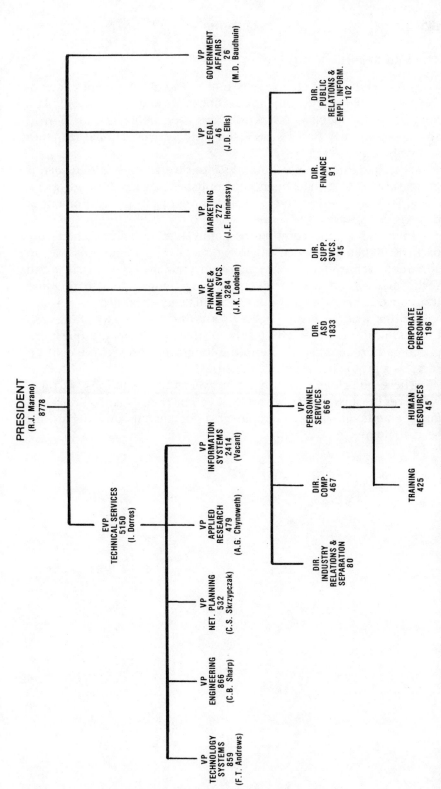

FIGURE 13. Bell Communications Research Corporation. (Note: headcount is indicated below each position title.)

The End Result

The end result of the extensive planning and development efforts of the presidential study group, the ad hoc task force, the regional planners, scores of special study teams, and especially, Marano, Dorros, and Looloian, may best be depicted in the organizational structure shown in Figure 13.

The chart, drawn only 2 months into divestiture's second year, is a measure of what had been accomplished: a fully formed operational staff prepared to serve the seven regions from the moment of divestiture forward.

In retrospect, this complete assembly, integration, and chartering of an 8800-person service organization in only 14 months was an admirable achievement, particularly in view of the fact that it had seven masters, often with divergent views, together with pressure from outside agencies that questioned its very existence.

At this writing, many people in the industry are watching Bell Communications Research closely, in the context of the questions posed earlier: first, is it viable in the long run? And second, could it serve as a prototype for other industries?

These questions can only be answered in the fullness of time. Whatever the answers, however, BCR will provide organizational and management gurus considerable grist for analysis and debate for years to come.

Chapter 4

Cultural Transformation

As complex and forbidding as were divestiture's other facets, many observers agreed that reshaping the corporate culture was ultimately the most difficult task confronting AT&T and the divested companies. The reason: the Bell System's culture was as broad as the enterprise itself; as pervasive and deeply rooted as any value system in American business; as amorphous, and yet as critical, as the attitudes, belief structures, and expectations of 1 million employees.

To effect legal, financial, operational, *and* psychological divestiture in ways that would assure continued success, the culture would have to be assessed, redefined, and adapted to bring the value systems and expectations of AT&T people into congruence with the corporation's new mission and to prepare employees for the aggressively competitive regions they were entering. It is only fair to add in this connection that Bell System people were already used to competition, though of a different character—a rivalry and testing that pitted company against company and department against department in achieving results based on internal indices that strictly measured performance in many categories. For so large an enterprise, in a regulated context, there was hardly another way, but it was still spirited and highly effective.

Nonetheless, as John Malone, a management consultant, noted in *The Wall Street Journal* of February 28,1984: "AT&T stands ready to mortgage its future if it doesn't reshape its culture to meet the new competitive battles ahead." However, this was a tall order indeed. No disciplined methodology, and almost no useful empirical data, existed for changing cultural elements. In fact, there does not yet appear to be a clear consensus on how to diagnose or measure culture within an organization. As *Fortune* reported in October 1983:

> A review of the evidence suggests that anybody who tries to unearth a corporation's culture, much less change it, is in for a rough time. The values and beliefs people espouse frequently tend to be half-hidden and elusive. Diagnosing culture calls for unusual, time-consuming techniques: auditing the content of decision-making, holding open-ended interviews with people ranging from the man working on the loading dock to the executive in the corner office.

WHAT IS CORPORATE CULTURE?

"A nation's culture," said Mahatma Gandhi, "resides in the heart and soul of its people." So with corporations. Like nations, corporations evolve distinct cultures from a rather complex interaction of factors, including past and present experiences, structural characteristics, and corporate leaders. Loosely defined, a company's culture is the amalgam of shared values, behavior patterns, mores, symbols, attitudes, and normative ways of conducting business that, more than its products or services, differentiate it from all other companies. Cultural uniqueness is a primary and cherished feature of organizations, a critical asset that is nurtured in the internal value system.

It is no exaggeration to observe that the corporate culture encompasses the very meaning of the organization, providing the metabolism and energy that drive it toward its strategic and tactical goals. Often, the culture accounts for the success of one company over a competitor possessed of equal talents and resources but inferior cultural strengths.

By coincidence, today's lively interest in the concept of organizational culture and its role in corporate fortunes reached a new intensity in the early 1980s. Observers had begun to postulate that culture may play as significant a role as either strategy or structure in long-term performance, *especially in the large corporate organization experiencing significant changes in its markets and/or business environment.* Then, quite unexpectedly, AT&T and the U.S. Department of Justice announced the MFJ consent agreement. And suddenly, cultural observers from academe, business, and the media had before them a living case study, a virtual laboratory of cultural change in real time—not only because of the radical nature of the change imposed but also because of the critically compressed time frame in which the change had to occur.

Of course, AT&T's transformation would not precisely anticipate cultural changes in other industries. Divestiture would forever stand as a unique business event whose features were unlikely ever to be duplicated. The numbers of people affected, the sheer size of divested resources, the nature of the network, and the historic service relationship between Bell and the nation were but some of the considerations that set it apart from other potential corporate rearrangements.

Nonetheless, divestiture provided an extraordinary opportunity for testing scores of cultural concepts, not least among them the contention of authors Terrence Deal and Allen Kennedy that the "business environment is the single greatest influence in shaping a corporate culture" (*Corporate Cultures: The Rites and Rituals of Corporate Life,* A&W Publishers, 1982). Beyond question, the change in business environments for AT&T bracketed the range of extremes, from a relatively quiescent, regulated environment to a very highly competitive one. Moreover, at the precise moment the corporation turned to face its own transformation, the telecommunications industry was starting to become an overheated, high-tech arena, with powerful foreign and domestic firms streaming into the marketplace. Because culture is so much at the center of organizational functioning, it is critical to adaptability. Small wonder, then, that when commenting on how the company was adapting to competition, Robert E. Allen, then AT&T's chief financial officer, said, "We have a cultural issue on our hands."

HISTORY AND HEROES

For decades, AT&T had enjoyed the benefits of an extraordinarily strong and productive culture, one deeply embedded in its history and its heroes. The culture was first exemplified by Theodore Vail, the principal architect of the Bell System, and later broadened and reinforced by succeeding generations of top managers.

Bell's traditional culture blended a constellation of mutually reinforcing features and attributes, the most prominent of which were lifetime careers, up-from-the-ranks management succession, dedication to customer service, operational skills, consensus management, level consciousness, and a strong focus on regulatory matters. (It is interesting to note that except for the "regulatory" attribute, these characteristics all track closely with the highly extolled virtues of Japanese corporate culture.)

All of these attributes evolved to directly support one superordinate goal: universal service. In fact, everything related to the culture was affected by this goal: the kind of people hired, their shared value systems, the infrastructure of processes to run the business. All were committed to the unchanging objective of providing high-quality service at affordable prices to everyone in the United States.

Rarely, in fact, had corporate mission and corporate culture been so ideally matched. However, with the dawning of the 1980s, it became clear that universal service had largely been achieved and that the regulated environment would rapidly give way to a competitive one.

On considering the possibilities, one AT&T editor enthused in *Bell Telephone Magazine* in March, 1983: "The balance of the decade crackles with entrepreneurial spirit, the years beyond are gravid with promise and challenge and, one is tempted to say, unparalleled excitement." However, to mobilize that spirit, certain bedrock values would have to be discarded, or at least reshaped and redirected. (This is not to say that a culture forged for a regulatory environment is inferior to one adapted to the competitive marketplace, any more than a sailboat is inferior to a powerboat. It says only that they are distinctly different from one another, mechanisms evolved for different purposes.)

As noted, many analysts considered negotiating these changes as one of the most important managerial undertakings in all of divestiture. In a 1984 issue of *AT&T Magazine* management authority Richard T. Pascale claimed, in fact, that "the primary task for AT&T leadership is to redefine its values—to identify 'magnetic north.'" He added, "You need not abandon old values in wholesale fashion; but values cannot retain their validity in the new environment unless they are reinterpreted in the context of the customer and the marketplace."

Indeed, certain aspects of the culture would have to be nurtured and protected through the great transition. These included, most prominently, AT&T's historic vision of fairness to employees, owners, and customers; its dedication to the service ethic; its mutually rein-forcing senses of loyalty and unity; its operational and technical skills and concern for safety standards. As Tony H. Bonaparte, dean of business at Pace University remarked in the same issue of *AT&T Magazine*, "All of these are of incalculable importance in lubricating sound human relationships which are so crucial to managing task assignment and teamwork in a complex and sophisticated modern organization." Other cultural attributes, however, would have to be adapted, even as the management addressed hidden cultural barriers to change.

PREDIVESTITURE BEGINNINGS: "MA BELL DOESN'T LIVE HERE ANYMORE"

To say that changing the organizational culture at AT&T was a result of divestiture is to misrepresent the facts. AT&T's adaptation to a steadily more competitive environment—the overarching motivation for cultural change—began in the mid-1970s. Divestiture served essentially to thrust the transition forward, compressing the time frame for change.

During the divestiture years, there was no failure of recognition that the culture would have to be adapted. Yet, as I pointed out in the fall 1983 *Sloan Management Review*, "No AT&T manager is charged specifically with the management of the corporate culture. No task force is studying its dimensions. No committee is planning approaches to altering its underlying aspects."

One reason, as suggested previously, was the breadth and depth of the organization's culture, which implied that not one but rather *all* managers must be responsible for changing it. A second reason was the enormity of effort required to pull off the breakup and the consequent demand on managerial time and energy, which itself all but precluded a formalized effort to redefine the culture. Perhaps the most important factor was that it was in the very nature of corporate culture to change by evolution rather than by edict. As Bob Kinkead of *AT&T Magazine* observed, a new corporate culture is like a new wine, with several developmental stages. "Rough manipulation will not improve it, nor will it benefit from benign neglect. Only through good judgment and delicate handling can it achieve its full promise."

Thus, cultural change would neither be easily nor quickly achieved, its importance notwithstanding. And while "rough manipulation" would indeed not achieve desired results, the culture could be positively influenced by consistent, thoughtful managerial action. As noted in the *Sloan Management Review* article, managing cultural change is a three-step process.

1. Management must understand the meaning and impact of corporate culture and must ascertain, largely through empirical methods, the elements of its own culture.

2. The cultural wheat must be separated from the chaff. Decisions must be made about which elements support future goals and strategies and must be retained, and which elements are no longer appropriate and must be changed.

3. Appropriate actions must be taken to effect the required changes in a way that leaves the desirable elements unaffected.

Since Bell's was a strong and mature culture whose relevance was well understood, the first of these steps required little overt action. The second, separating wheat from chaff, however, entailed a pervasive effort that was necessitated by the shift from a regulated to a competitive environment. (Such a shift required basic changes not only in the ways AT&T people thought about doing business but also in the ways that business was done. Thus, the changes reverberated intensely throughout the corporation.) The third step, taking action, was the most dramatic. As described in subsequent pages, whole series of actions were in fact taken that were literally without parallel in the history of AT&T.

The process of change was entirely a conscious one. In a *Bell Telephone Magazine* article in 1982, AT&T's board chairman summed up both the objective and its importance: "If we are able to adapt our marvelous culture to a different environment—and if we remember that the business in the '80s cannot be run by memory—we can set the course for the next century."

Actually, signs of conscious cultural change could be perceived long before the divestiture announcement. Even before assuming the chairmanship, for example, Chairman Brown began to express new concepts for a new era. In a talk before the Commercial Club of Chicago in 1978, he pointed out, "There is a new telephone company in town, a high technology business applying advanced marketing strategies." In that same talk, he asked his audience to pass the word—

inside and outside the Bell System—that "Ma Bell doesn't live here anymore."

Early in the 1980s, changes in the corporate infrastructure began to appear. Revised management systems, new recruiting objectives and overhauled compensation schemes began to edge the corporate body toward a competitive attitude.

Through the 24 months of divestiture planning, cultural change accelerated. As marketplace uncertainty replaced regulatory uncertainty, AT&T managers placed ever greater emphasis on shifting the corporate mindset toward a competitive orientation. Strategic planning for the first time began to employ competitive analytical techniques. A functional organizational structure moved further toward market-segmented lines-of-business structures. Costing and pricing methodologies moved from a basis of cross-subsidies and national price averaging to product-by-product and service-by-service computation schemes.

No less important, the corporate value system began to recognize and reward a more entrepreneurial type of manager than in the past. AT&T's people were suddenly being urged more toward risk taking than care taking, a fact made clear by Chairman Brown in several key speeches.

Throughout the firestorm of divestiture, employees at all levels made change, specifically including organizational change, a part of their systems of expectations. "The essence of this organization is not found in corporate names or boundaries," Chairman Brown assured them in a talk before the Pioneer General Assembly in September 1983. "It is found in the people and the spirit of those aggregations. And they will be as vital and dynamic as ever."

LOOKING BACK TO SEE AHEAD: A MORE FOCUSED APPROACH

In late 1983 when it became clear that divestiture could, in fact, be achieved by January 1 (doubts remained virtually to the end), AT&T's management could breathe a collective sigh of relief and turn its attention more to the human side of the enterprise. The initiative began at the very top. In early December, shortly after AT&T President Bill Ellinghaus announced his plans to retire several months hence, Chairman Brown asked him to look into the matter of cultural change. In typically succinct style, he asked Ellinghaus to find answers to one central question: "Have we adequately addressed the impact of divestiture on our culture and our people?"

The stated objective was "to provide senior management with the means not only to understand the dislocations and strains caused by divestiture, but also to determine what new initiatives may be required to adapt current cultural values to the new environment." The chairman requested that Ellinghaus provide the answers by February 15, the latter's last day in office. (The regional companies were invited to "piggyback" on the methodology AT&T would develop for diagnosing cultural impact, on a "for your eyes only" basis. They declined, underscoring their newly found independence.)

The chairman's charge to Ellinghaus sent a signal throughout the new AT&T that attention to cultural change—more precisely, adaptation of behavior patterns to the new environment—had taken its place as a high-order priority.

THE STUDY

As mentioned previously, no generally accepted conceptual model exists for diagnosis of corporate cultural elements. Thus, when I was assigned the study for staff direction, I had to custom-design an approach.

Ultimately, the study comprised three elements, to assure that all bases were covered. First, Bill Ellinghaus wrote a personal request to twenty key executives in the company for their assessments of divestiture's impact on AT&T's culture and for their recommendations. Second, interviews were conducted with several outside management consultants familiar with Bell's history and current situation. Among them were such well-known experts as Michael Maccoby, Stanley Peterfreund, Harry Levinson, and Frank Stanek. Third, a comprehensive survey was made of a scientifically selected sample of employees across the corporation, seeking answers from the "soul" of the organization.

The response was extraordinary. Each of the queried executives wrote a carefully considered and highly detailed memorandum, more than a few of which reflected the pain of divestiture they had witnessed and felt. The interviews with the consultants also provided important perspectives. However, the richest sources of all proved to be the responses to the employee questionnaire, from which measurable patterns of attitudes and reactions could be discerned for the corporation as a whole and for each subsidiary unit. In fact, a larger percentage of employees responded to the survey, without any follow-up prompting, than had answered any other survey in the corporation's extensive history of employee opinion sampling.

To the degree possible, the wealth of information gathered from these three assessments was quantified and computerized so that it could be examined along many lines of inquiry. Then all data were subjected to in-depth review and analysis. The results were as revealing in their consistency as in their considerable substance.

Bill Ellinghaus ended his outstanding 44-year career in the Bell System on the afternoon of February 15, just after the AT&T board of directors meeting. His last contribution as AT&T's president was to deliver to the board chairman the full report of the culture study, briefing him on its substance. His tenure with Bell had been so characterized by concern for the company's constituencies—and most especially, the welfare of its people—that ending with a sensitive and caring analysis of the culture seemed especially fitting.

The Findings: Bad News, Good News

Not surprisingly, key executives, knowledgeable outsiders, and the rank and file all saw divestiture as a high-impact event on employees and on their shared value system—their collective culture. The data yielded literally hundreds of observations and conclusions, and along virtually every important dimension the information was mutually reinforcing.

Of course, differences were perceived between employment levels, between organizational units, between the so-called subcultures. But with regard to AT&T's overarching cultural attributes, there was a consistency of response. Below are summarized what were seen to be the five major findings of the Ellinghaus study:

1. The shock attendant upon the breakup and the subsequent burdensome workload to implement an order felt to be wrong for the company, the customer, and the nation at large took a heavy toll on AT&T people. A high percentage said they had found it physically and emotionally taxing and felt it had taken too much time from their families.

2. There was an almost overwhelming concern among employees everywhere regarding AT&T's ability to continue to provide high-

quality service, given the demise of end-to-end responsibility caused by the MFJ, and the possible "drag" toward service mediocrity resulting from prospective price wars.

3. The collective confidence of the employee body had been badly shaken by the divestiture experience. Consequently, employees tended to feel less secure about their jobs (a realistic concern, to be sure), and about their career opportunities in what they rightly perceived as a new ball game.

4. Employees wondered about AT&T's ability to compete, given the newness of the competitive environment and the remnant regulatory constraints still imposed.

5. Encouragingly, employees recognized and accepted the need for a new priority of attributes, with regard to characteristics most vital to the future success of the company. For example, market aggressiveness, technological innovation, profitability, and fast response to customer needs outranked company loyalty, lifetime careers, up-from-the-ranks management succession, consensus management, and community involvement—all high fliers in the regulated environment of yesteryear. (It was seen as heartening that these new values were precisely the ones senior management believed should be emphasized. Many people had already begun to make the shift.)

Summing up, there was a corporate identity crisis if sorts immediately after the divestiture experience. A collective voice could almost be heard to say: "I knew the old Bell System, its mission, its operation, its people, its culture. And I knew my niche in it. In that knowledge, I had identity and confidence about my company and myself. Now I work for a new company, one-fourth its former size, with only a partial history and no track record. With the loss of our mission and the fragmentation of telephone service, I find myself asking, Who are we? Who am I?"

The good news was that despite this transitory identity problem, a pervasive excitement and anticipation about the "new ball game" radiated throughout the answers to the survey. Furthermore, an abiding pride in being a member of AT&T was crowned with the belief that it would still be a winner if given time and a "level playing field" by Washington.

In short, AT&T people had been bruised but not broken—not by a long shot.

Question 13

Transcending and more revealing than all the results of the quantified statistical data was the qualitative aspect rendered as a result of one question asked of employees on the questionnaire. It was question 13, the last:

What were *your* feelings as the new year and the new AT&T era dawned on January 1, 1984? Feel free to share your thoughts, about the passing of the old Bell System, the birth of the new AT&T and its impact on you as you begin work this year.

The emotional response exceeded anything AT&T's professional attitude surveyors had ever seen. Question 13 had been included as a kind of catch-all item, to pick up anything that the other questions failed to evoke. But more than 3400 respondents (57 per cent of all employees who received questionnaire forms—statistically a remarkable percentage) took time to describe their feelings and experiences, often in considerable detail. It was as if they had been waiting for an opportunity to tell someone in authority of their sadness, anger, even outrage at divestiture, and of their pride in their heritage and their tentative hopes and optimism about the future.

By sampling some of the responses it is possible to provide a unique sense of what AT&T employees (and, we suspect, those in the regional companies, too) felt about the corporate trauma called divestiture. Here are a few randomly selected excerpts:

- Angry, sad, a little scared about my future. Divestiture was a triumph of lawyers, bureaucrats, and financial manipulators over producers and servers.

- I felt like I had gone through a divorce that neither my wife nor my children wanted. It was forced upon us by some very powerful outside force and I could not control the outcome. It was like waking up in familiar surroundings (your home) but your family and all that you held dear was missing.

- I felt sad and somewhat resentful because the government has been absolutely wrong on the question of competition. Foreign telephone companies think the U.S. is crazy for breaking up AT&T. . . . Yet I think young managers will see challenge and opportunities.

- A sense of loss; we were screwed by the Federal Government.

- My feelings were ambivalent . . . I was numb but I neither rejoiced nor shed a tear. The old AT&T and the operating companies were great places to work. The new AT&T will also be a good place to work. With so many people with such a long standing ethic of quality of service, it can't help be that.

- Working through divestiture was exciting, challenging and hard, productive work. The aftermath has been a letdown. Once the estate is settled, things may sort out.

The comments speak for themselves. But significantly, through the anger and frustration shone a strong resolve, a commitment to get on with the management of the new company.

MR. BROWN TAKES CHARGE

In all the literature on corporate culture, one tenet is shared by theoreticians and practitioners alike: cultural change must be led from the top. AT&T was no exception. Almost 18 months before the survey, Chairman Brown had described the corporate culture to an audience at the Harvard Business School, in September 1982, and explained that "though corporate strategies can be recast overnight, a corporate culture cannot be laid aside like an old suit that is no longer considered stylish." He added that "our job now is to adapt that culture to changing times and different needs. The challenge will be to change our culture without changing the character of our business." Now, with the Ellinghaus report in hand, the chairman moved to meet that challenge. He began by transmitting copies of the Ellinghaus report to the top fifteen officers of AT&T, his so-called cabinet. The cover note apprised them of a special meeting, and signaled its importance. "I am interrupting my vacation for this meeting," the note read. "We clearly have work to do."

The meeting, held in early March 1984, comprised a frank discussion of divestiture's impact on the corporation's people, the steps that had been taken to date in adapting the culture, and further initiatives that might be needed. It was all extremely fruitful, not only in providing the substance for cultural change but also in involving the support of the top executive team in the change process.

There was no rhetorical fanfare about the Ellinghaus report, no broad pronouncements about cultural change to the employee body. However, the report had helped senior management to take action, and thus accomplished its purpose. In fact, the actions taken struck squarely at employees' major concerns, as revealed in the Ellinghaus study, actions aimed at reestablishing a sense of mission, identity, confidence, and self-renewal after the distress of divestiture.

Some of the principal informational steps taken included the following:

- Broad-scale distribution of a talk by Chairman Brown entitled *A New Vision for AT&T*, in which he articulated the new mission (to universalize the information age), outlined new strategies and aims, and discussed how the style of management had to change for the company to succeed in the new environment.

- Company-wide transmission of videotapes featuring a panel of top corporate officers, including the chairman, answering questions from employees about the new AT&T.

- A series of in-house publications featuring articles on the new AT&T, the titles of which make clear their thrust. For example:

  - *AT&T: One Enterprise, One Mission, One Measure*

  - *Corporate Headquarters, Owner and Manager*

  - *No One Will Show You the Way*

- A sequence of talks by officers to AT&T audiences, incorporating the new vision, goals, and desired performance (for example, bias to action, risk taking, individual initiative, etc.)

- The announcement of a new, 1-week corporate seminar for the top 800 executives, designed to develop a total understanding of the new company and its environment. Top executives would appear each week for dialogue on the corporation's identity and mission and the challenges it faces. Management style and expectations would be major seminar topics as well.

- One document, designed for release in mid-1984, was developed to provide a comprehensive depiction of AT&T's new organization, the roles and relationships between the various units, underlying principles and values, and finally, the major decision processes—all critical contributors to the corporate culture. The document, entitled *AT&T's Management System*, was designed to increase employees' level of understanding and knowledge of how the new AT&T functions and, hence, to develop a better sense of "who we are."

- One sector declared a "war" on needless red tape and bureaucracy and set up a control center to receive, evaluate, and, where feasible, implement employee suggestions.

- Several units began formal recognition of outstanding achievements in matters that encouraged new behavior (for example, an Eagle Award for marketing ideas or super sales; a Golden Boy award for exemplary customer service; a cost-reduction program aimed at providing cash-equivalent awards for accepted ideas on cutting costs).

- An advertising program (directed to all AT&T constituencies) was equally effective in aiding the change process inside the corporation. The outstanding ads created—designed to portray AT&T as a quality information and communications competitor—reinforced the internal initiatives, promoting among employees a new sense of identity and pride.

SIGNS OF CHANGE

It has been observed that cultural change cannot be delegated to the human resources or employee information departments, that indeed substantive change grows much more directly and predictably out of what the corporation does than what it says.

Unquestionably, the actions outlined above helped to achieve much-needed adaptation in employee views and values. However, the transforming and sometimes extraordinary actions of the corporation—most especially in the 12-month period bracketing the effective date of divestiture—also had significant impact on the culture.

The few examples outlined below are culled from a much longer list. Their purpose is to show a changing predisposition toward competitive behavior for the corporation as a whole—perhaps the most significant indicator of all of productive cultural adaptations.

INTERNAL CHANGE

August 1983 AT&T announces new corporate identity, mission, and organizational structure.

November 1983 AT&T offers early retirement package to 13,000 people to streamline force.

December 1983 AT&T Technologies organizes into six new lines of business, creating profit center management groups along market and product lines.

March 1984 AT&T Consumer Products consolidates repair operations to gain efficiencies and meet customer needs.

May 1984 AT&T petitions the FCC to speed up depreciation of equipment, "a practice required in the competitive world."

June 1984 Jim Olson, AT&T vice chairman, goes on closed-circuit TV throughout the company, nationwide, to announce immediate 20 percent cost reduction program.

July 1984 For the first time in its history, AT&T announces a freeze on the salary structure of all its managers—a move affecting 114,000 employees.

August 1984 In connection with the 20 percent cost reduction program, AT&T announces that 11,000 positions will be eliminated in the AT&T Technologies sector.

October 1984 AT&T Technologies moves further toward consolidating and vertically integrating lines of business.

October 1984 AT&T offers early retirement to many senior officers.

JOINT VENTURES

August 1983 AT&T and Phillips of the Netherlands enter into joint-venture agreement to market switching and transmission equipment in Europe.

September 1983 AT&T Communications and Netcom Enterprises win multimillion-dollar contract from European Broadcasting Union to provide broadcast of Olympic games throughout Europe.

November 1983	AT&T establishes links to Wang and Hewlett-Packard to produce compatible computer equipment (first time).
December 1983	AT&T buys 25 percent stake in Olivetti to distribute and manufacture each others' products.
January 1984	Digital Equipment agrees to use AT&T's UNIX software for mid- and high-range VAX computers.
March 1984	AT&T Information Systems joins Rockwell International, Honeywell, and Data General on finding ways for computers to swap data with telephone switching equipment.
August 1984	AT&T and Spain's Compañía Telefónica Nacional agree to form a joint-venture company to design and manufacture custom-integrated circuits in Spain.
	AT&T announces creation of a joint-venture company, AT&T Taiwan Telecommunications, Inc., to manufacture and market advanced digital switching systems.

NEW PRODUCTS AND SERVICES

October 1983	AT&T adapts Number 5 Electronic Switch for international customers.
October 1983	AT&T Information Systems announces first new product specifically designed for small-business market: Merlin Communications System.
November 1983	AT&T unveils new "Caller Card" phone, which uses card instead of voice or dialing card number.
March 1984	AT&T Technologies enters computer marketplace with 3B family. Five mini- and microcomputers are broadest introduction in industry's history.
March 1984	AT&T Communications begins offering long-distance discount programs.
March 1984	AT&T Information Systems introduces System 75 for small offices.
June 1984	AT&T Technologies unveils its first personal computer in a joint venture with Olivetti of Italy.

These illustrations are, as indicated, merely samples of a much broader front of new initiatives within AT&T. Significantly, not one of them would have been in the Bell System works as little as 3 years previously. However, new competitive indicators were suddenly becoming almost routine. Indeed, people saw clearly that Ma Bell did not live here anymore.

Despite all the dramatic evidence of adaptation, it would be inaccurate to portray the scene as an overnight and total cultural transformation. What the listing represents is a change in the perspectives of top leadership. To assume that the entire corporate body of more than 350,000 people had arrived at a new orientation would be far off the mark. As James J. O'Toole noted in *Making America Work: Productivity and Responsibility* (Continuum, 1981), culture change "is a pluralistic process, not a monolithic one." It will take time—considerable time—for the new values to permeate throughout the new AT&T. But the start at the top was an encouraging and productive one, bearing witness to the assertion that the company was, as its ads proclaimed, "reaching out in new directions."

By mid-1984, divestiture began to fade. It was not forgotten, of course, any more than the traditional Bell System heritage could be forgotten, but, of necessity, left behind. As one writer observed, organizations, like people, often deal best with loss by moving on. What lay ahead was the exciting challenge of creating the next stage of AT&T's long history. That challenge required that AT&T adapt itself as successfully to the competitive environment as it did to the regulatory one.

To do so—and at the same time to change our culture without changing the character of our business—would not only serve customers and shareholders, but also pay tribute to millions of Bell employees of decades past who dedicated themselves to the achievement of universal service. Thus, a successful transition would serve a dual celebration: commemoration of the corporation's enduring heritage and commitment to its new and exciting future.

Chapter 5

Lessons Learned:
Managing the Transition

In retrospect, it is clear that the process of managing divestiture was, on balance, remarkably successful. Judged by many as one of the most formidable management challenges in American business history, divestiture was accomplished in minimal time, with the least possible impact upon the corporation's constituencies, and with no major disruption in the nation's telephone service. Not that the project proceeded without false starts, reversals, stalemates, and debates; indeed, it was riddled with them. However, from today's vantage point, the fact that the breakup was achieved in the allotted time is itself testimony to the fact that the divestiture management approach was an effective one.

What can be learned, then, from the experience? Is there a measure of practical knowledge to be gleaned from this extraordinary event, knowledge that may be useful to others engaged in managing change and, most especially, to those charged with managing corporate transmigrations to new business environments?

The answer, with two provisions, is that useful lessons abound. First, it must be borne in mind, in analyzing and applying the lessons of divestiture, how exceptional an event this was. If institutional

161

adaptation is surveyed, along with the extent of change, the speed with which it occurred, its complexity, and the degree of uncertainty attendant upon it, then it becomes clear that the Bell System divestiture was a unique event. Under the pressures of the divestiture mandate, Bell managers functioned in a virtual laboratory of radical change; uncertainty was a constant companion to their decisions. Indeed, it is arguable that no corporation in history has been required to make so sweeping a transformation in so short a time.

Does this mean that divestiture's lessons are inapplicable for other institutions—or somehow less than useful to decision makers of the future? On the contrary. Although the Bell System's transformation represents the most extreme dimensions of change, its lessons will nonetheless be useful and applicable to a broad array of companies whose managements, as a function of operating in today's changing business environment, face periods of prolonged uncertainty and complex adaptation.

The second provision or qualification is that while divestiture was rich in new managerial experiences, it did not yield unique and revolutionary management principles. Rather, it served as an unusually vivid clarification and confirmation of a number of principles already known to experienced executives. In fact, the effectiveness of some techniques, as well as the adverse impact of others, was exemplified and dramatized to a degree rare in most business case studies. The divestiture experience, then, served *to test and validate* rather than to *revolutionize* management theory.

Therefore, it is possible that the following observations on managing change will be helpful to a wide diversity of companies. Let it just be said first that in the interests not merely of corporate stability but, indeed, of national stability, it is hoped that few traumas on the order of divestiture are in store for us. It is further hoped, however, that if radical change should come, some of the lessons posited here will help guide those responsible for managing their own transitions.

LESSON 1: DON'T WAIT FOR CLARITY

Mobilize early.

In times of rapid change, waiting for all uncertainties to be resolved and all issues clarified is at best an exercise in futility, at worst a barrier to progress. It is much more productive to begin mobilizing for action immediately, even if some actions have to be modified later, since the very process of initiating momentum will prove a valuable energizing force.

In the divestiture situation, top management provided this initial stimulus. Indeed, as reported in a 1982 *Bell Telephone Magazine*:

> Hardly had the ink dried on the Modification of Final Judgment announced January 8 than the Bell System went to work building a new avenue to a new age. Broad organizational changes in AT&T's General Departments were announced January 21. The corporation's top four executives would devote themselves as a group to corporate strategy, resource allocation and critical issues. Day-to-day responsibilities would be handled by five executive vice presidents. Barely two weeks later, six study groups, comprised mostly of operating company presidents, were established.

Scores of other actions were taken in parallel. However, none better exemplified the productiveness of prompt action than the early formation of the study groups. This managerial initiative, perhaps more than any other, helped generate a momentum of activity that enabled the staff to deal with new issues as they developed.

Trust your instincts.

Where precedents are nonexistent and options are not clearcut, senior managers are wise to rely on their instincts and experience. No AT&T officer, obviously, had prior experience in divestiture management. Yet the six major issues defined very early in the game and assigned to the presidents' study groups turned out in the long run to be the core of the crucial questions of divestiture. Senior executives found that the concerns and preoccupations of recent years, combined with long managerial experience, had equipped them well to deal with the unfamiliar exigencies of divestiture.

Start with "best guess" assumptions.

The value of developing a set of best-guess assumptions at the outset of transition cannot be overemphasized. Such assumptions, widely circulated with the caveat that they are provisional, can break the paralysis that derives from feeling overwhelmed by uncertainty and complexity. They can free people for action and provide them with a construct against which to measure their responses.

Chapter 2 described the enormous usefulness of the first-draft assumption set, provided unbidden, by an AT&T middle manager. This initiative, whose importance cannot be overstated, went a long way toward overcoming inertia and moving the project forward on a wide front at the staff level. Equally decisive, it stimulated debate and surfaced issues between departments that could be escalated for resolution.

One caution: the assumption set should be viewed as a flexible instrument, not a rigid doctrine. It should be subject to constant change as complexities become better understood and uncertainty diminishes.

LESSON 2: DELEGATE RESPONSIBILITY WHEREVER POSSIBLE

As familiar a principle to seasoned managers as delegation is, it is one most dramatically proven by the divestiture experience. Throughout that experience, the evidence was abundant that, given the freedom and authority to act, people will rise to meet even the most awesome challenges. Again, the manager who seized the moment in preparing the assumptions is an ideal model of what can be expected.

It is a principle that perhaps bears considerable repetition, simply because of the natural tendency of supervisors to keep close control of all activity under their jurisdictions. In the Bell System, moreover, this tendency was reinforced by a long tradition of cautious, deliberate decison making, with multiple sign-offs at high levels.

In a regulatory setting, it was an appropriate and prudent tradition. Divestiture, however, made this sort of procedure not only inappropriate but impossible. The magnitude, the complexity, and the tight deadlines virtually forced a delegation of responsibility down the line: even managers who may have preferred tight control could not possibly have achieved it.

For the divestiture project there was, therefore, a massive shift of normal authority and responsibility down the organizational line throughout AT&T. The effectiveness of response by the many employees thus empowered can be gauged by the extraordinary end result—successful divestiture, on time.

Push down implementation (not policy) decisions.

Major policy matters, of course, must remain the domain of senior management. But on thousands of questions as to precisely *how* divestiture would be implemented, decisions were delegated to middle and lower levels. This is as it should be.

On the matter of personnel transfers, to cite one example, guiding principles were established at the outset—namely, "People will follow their work" and "Force surpluses and shortages will be shared among all entities." It was then left to managers at lower levels to determine specific allocation ratios and transfer assignments. These and other principles set off a cascade of efforts down the line to develop personnel allocation methodology, negotiating procedures between parties, and person-specific assignment details.

Provide maximum leeway for independent thinkers and subject-matter experts.

Even in tranquil times, a corporation gains greatly from a management structure and style that allow productive autonomy for subject-matter experts and problem solvers down the line. In times of upheaval, this becomes an absolute essential. The energy and creativity of knowledgeable and original thinkers at all levels throughout the organization will often provide the key contributions to successful transition—contributions that could never have come through conventional bureaucratic channels.

The critical importance of such contributions was detailed throughout earlier chapters. In hundreds of areas, the corporation was dependent on the expertise and judgment of the SMEs. Incalculable benefit was derived from allowing them to work with executives on the divestiture guidelines, with lawyers on the Plan of Reorganization, and with one another on problems that crossed departmental boundaries.

LESSON 3: SET OVERALL GUIDELINES AT THE TOP

Delegation of authority is essential in carrying out a complex transition. But delegated activity will be successful only if it occurs in the context of clear principles and guidelines established at the top.

It has been stressed that the supervisory impulse to maintain tight personal control over all aspects of a job can be counterproductive where rapid change is needed. Other kinds of control, however, are necessary to keep decentralized activities coordinated in the direction of common goals. In times of change, a set of clearly formulated general principles will provide such controls far more effectively than constant "hands-on" managerial direction. If the major elements of policy are agreed upon at the top and thoroughly understood down the line, there is a good chance that even a multitude of widespread and diverse decisions and projects will evolve in harmony, rather than at cross purposes.

Sometimes, of course, well-known precedent can serve to provide such guidelines. In the case of divestiture, however, neither precedent nor corporate analogue existed. Broad, guiding principles, formulated fairly early in the process, were necessary to orient all parts of the massive effort. The most basic of these principles were articulated early on by the chairman in a message to Bell System people. They were, essentially, the four overarching guidelines for divestiture:

- First, to the extent humanly possible, our services to all segments of the public will be provided at the same or better levels than have been the hallmark of the Bell System.

- Second, the integrity of the investment of the 3.2 million owners of the business will be preserved.

- Third, the reorganization will be carried out in such a way as to ensure that you—the people of the Bell System—will have employment security and continued career opportunity.

- And fourth, the divested companies will be launched with the management, financial, technical, and physical resources necessary to make them flourishing enterprises in the regions in which they will operate.

Other principles emanated from the presidents' study groups, in part distilled from the assumption set. They served as guideposts of policy throughout the divestiture project, surfacing in internal planning documents and eventually becoming formalized in the Plan of Reorganization.

Provide a mechanism for rapid escalation of stalemated issues.

Achieving a successful balance between delegation and top-level control depends considerably on the procedures for handling stalemates down the line. Accessible channels and structures must be provided for escalating issues that cannot be satisfactorily resolved at lower ranks. Although this is clearly important during corporate business-as-usual, it becomes paramount when demands for rapid change cannot tolerate time lost to deadlocked issues.

In the divestiture process, issue escalation was facilitated most prominently by the issue-tracking and monitoring activities under the officer responsible for divestiture planning and implementation, Vice President Bill Sharwell. In addition, the infrastructure of boards and committees, including the Restructure Implementation Board (RIB), provided other channels to top management, particularly on matters relating to the unfolding day-to-day events on the legal, legislative, and regulatory fronts and on issues rising from within the massive AT&T-BOC staff effort.

LESSON 4: COMMUNICATE WHAT IS KNOWN AND WHAT IS STILL UNKNOWN, WIDELY AND OFTEN

Where uncertainties abound, employees need to know where things stand. Responding to this need—promptly, regularly, and forthrightly—is not only good psychology but also adds immeasurably to the common base of knowledge for moving the project forward.

Throughout divestiture, AT&T's employee communications organization provided a torrent of information on a daily basis. External events affecting divestiture, as well as internal status reports on every aspect of the project, were covered in depth and broadly disseminated. Newsletters, management reports, closed-circuit forums featuring key personnel, speeches, and *Bell Telephone Magazine* articles all combined to keep AT&T people abreast of the saga they were sharing.

After divestiture, surveys verified that employees felt the information flow on divestiture was timely, accurate, and helpful to them in the conduct of their work. In fact, to a surprising extent, the corporation's rank and file used this media output as a tracking device for matters affecting their own sphere of responsibility. Having assumed responsibility for their "piece of the action," they were keen to avoid roadblocks and thus on the lookout for anything that would deter their efforts. Often, the employee information program would provide grist for intense issue-oriented debate between parties. In the absence of this catalyst, the issue would have risen at a later date, perhaps resulting in a loss of time and even jeopardy of the critical 1/1/84 deadline.

It should be noted that communicating good news and bad, promptly and honestly, did not reflect a new value within AT&T. In fact, it was institutionalized in the corporate belief system as early as 1911, when then-president Theodore Vail wrote: "It is not only the right but the obligation of all individuals, or aggregations of individuals, who come before the public, to see that the public has full and correct information." However, the crucible of change that was divestiture served to magnify and to reconfirm both the truth and the utility of this principle—most especially as it related to the employee "public."

LESSON 5: SET FIRM TARGET DATES

America is a time-oriented society. Consultants specialize in time management; broadcasters aim for 30-second news coverage; joggers brag of "personal best time." "Commute time" is cocktail talk, and the 1-minute manager may be our closest thing to a national hero. In the work place, this acute time consciousness makes the target date a serious matter. A missed target date can be punishable by corporate death—by dismissal or, more commonly, relegation to the managerial deadwood pile.

It is inarguably true, then, that time pressures can have destructive effects. Indeed, not for nothing is the image of the deadline-tormented manager a familiar stereotype of corporate life. Clearly, care needs to be exercised in applying such pressures. By the same token, there are positive aspects to the phenomena that deserve more attention than they have received. First among them is that time pressure can serve as a stimulating—even exhilarating—impetus to action.

Witness, as a prime example, the Bell System divestiture. The judgment to make the break on January 1, 1984—instead of the somewhat later date permitted—came from the top very soon after the settlement agreement was reached in January 1982. That decision, which left less than 2 years for the task, was based on both practical and psychological factors. For one thing, having divestiture coincide with the start of a new year would minimize the complexities of the mammoth auditing and accounting jobs involved with transfers of assets and people. For another, it was recognized that dismantling the system would cause substantial psychic pain, and that to ease the time constraint would also be to prolong the pain.

To set a date beyond January 1, 1984, might indeed have been counter-productive. Accordingly, Chairman Brown opted for a deadline that seemed virtually impossible to meet. In retrospect, it was the right decision. The pressure galvanized the entire organization into levels of activity no one could have imagined possible.

Use immovable targets to challenge, not intimidate.

The spectre of "one-one-eighty-four" on the horizon did not give rise to panic. Instead, throughout the company, people paced themselves accordingly. Thousands of intermediate deadlines sprang up and were met, surpassed, and replaced. Target dates proliferated and multiplied, raising the organizational temperature to a fever of productive activity.

It is very doubtful that divestiture could have been accomplished without such pervasive time pressures. To be sure, they induced tension and exhaustion. But they also unlocked reserves of energy and stamina, both individual and collective, unprecedented in the corporation's history.

During the transition, as noted, AT&T bulletin boards displayed a sign announcing that "adrenalin flows in direct proportion to the proximity of the completion date." High adrenalin at AT&T was sustained by the universal knowledge that the completion date was immovable and the mandate irrevocable. With that clarity, everyone rose to the unthinkable—and met the deadline.

LESSON 6: SEND A TOP-DOWN MESSAGE OF CONFIDENCE

When the corporate ship is turned in midcourse and instructed to pursue a radically different direction, corporate leaders are bound to spend some time searching for magnetic north. At the same time, the crew urgently needs reassurance from the top that the ship is under control. Difficult as it is to foster confidence at such times, the success of the new venture may depend upon it.

The salient communication is not "There are no problems"— such patent foolishness undermines credibility—but rather "We can solve the problems." The confidence of a top leader is a potent force. If he or she believes "they can do it," the likelihood increases that they actually can.

During the divestiture process, AT&T's top management, particularly the board chairman, made a point of remaining highly visible, addressing employees frequently, answering questions, and providing encouragement. It is hard to imagine a successful divestiture without such support.

Believe the message.

Although top officers' encouragement may conceal some doubts, it should constitute neither deliberate deception nor whistling in the dark. Their messages will only be effective if they themselves believe them to be true. Even if they wonder how the challenge will be handled, they must be firm in their conviction that their people are capable of rising to it. It is only this personal conviction on the part of a leader that is credible to employees, and that can inspire them to self-confidence.

Communicate new values.

When culture shock accompanies organizational change, messages from the top must combine avowals of confidence with expressions of the new cultural values. Encouragement to succeed should go hand in hand with clarification of new definitions of success.

Previous chapters have underscored the pivotal importance of cultural change in Bell System divestiture. The change struck at the heart of corporate and employee identity. And with the sudden obsolescence of traditional values, the sense of a loss of identity was threatening indeed.

Top executives recognized the importance of moving swiftly to backfill the void. Chapter 4 described in some detail the diverse ways in which the company attempted to provide new ideals, new sources of identity, and pride. The rapid switch from one value system to another was, of course, traumatic for many. But it is probable that a prolonged period of unfixed, undefined identity would have been far more destructive to morale.

CONCLUSION

These guidelines may appear to have been ordained at the start of the divestiture—consciously set in place at the first stage rather than evolving as the project proceeded. As noted earlier, this was not the case. Only looking back now can we reconstruct the model that unfolded in early 1982. And only looking back can we see how appropriate were the loose-knit, delegative management structures operating with the "invisible hand" of guiding principles.

Chapter 6

Lessons Learned: Managing Before and After

The preceding chapter has explored the process of managing divestiture itself, in the hope of culling from that experience some general guidelines on the management of transition. The principles outlined therein can apply to many sorts of corporate change: they are, or mean to be, generic to the management of transition. They do not address the question of transition from what to what?

The present chapter, in contrast, will focus on the specific nature of the change that AT&T experienced. Having concentrated on the dynamics of the change process itself, we will now explore the management implications of the particular kind of transformation undertaken by AT&T—namely, the change from a regulatory to a competitive business environment.

There has been relatively little attention paid by management literature to this phenomenon. Yet for the corporate manager it represents one of the most profound challenges in today's business world, requiring a massive reorientation of outlook and an overhaul of managerial structure, style, and practice.

AT&T's heritage was that of a highly regulated industry. After divestiture, although a considerable degree of regulation continued for AT&T, the company faced a marketplace competitive in the extreme. For managers, this did not entail simply a recalibration of existing procedures. It meant rather that few of the old procedures were germane at all in the new setting. It meant that every aspect of received wisdom had to be questioned, altered, and, if necessary, utterly recast.

Conventional theory has it that the competitive arena is far more demanding than a regulatory environment. And indeed no one would deny that it involves greater risk. But a regulatory regime poses demands of its own, often of considerable magnitude. Chapter 1 of this chronicle has highlighted the prolonged frustrations and difficulties experienced by AT&T's senior management while the company was under siege by various governmental regulatory agencies during the late 1970s and early 1980s.

Whether the demands on management under such conditions are more or less formidable than those faced by competitive companies is not only impossible to determine but also irrelevant to pursue. The pertinent question is not which of the two situations is harder but rather how they differ. For the fact is that they require and generate entirely different management systems, styles, and cultures. Much more can be gained by understanding the differences than by debating the merits of one or the other, especially as the issue is by no means confined to the telephone industry. The swings of the pendulum between regulatory oversight and rule by marketplace have carried many major industries on a volatile course in recent years and will continue to do so for the foreseeable future.

What AT&T has learned about the implications of this issue for managers may find resonance and response, therefore, in many quarters, although much more, clearly, remains to be learned.

BACKDROP TO CHANGE

It has been noted earlier that AT&T's entire tradition of management and corporate culture was rooted deeply in Theodore Vail's mission of universal service. That concept formed the basis for AT&T's strategic direction for more than half a century. The Bell System's entire infrastructure evolved and adapted accordingly over decades, always geared to that singular and powerful vision. Financial policy, technological development, pricing philosophy, market and product strategies, and organization design were complementary parts of a strategic orientation evolved for a regulatory world.

In adapting to a new world of competitive challenge, the company had to forge a new mission and a new decision-making infrastructure. In the process, every one of the strategic components so beautifully matched to the old environment had to be entirely reconceived and reformulated.

GENERAL STRATEGIC ORIENTATION

For the predivestiture Bell System, success was largely dependent upon convincing the Federal Communications Commission and the forty-eight state commissions of the need for adequate earnings (see Figure 14). Strategic thinking focused primarily on that specific objective, and the regulatory mindset was institutionalized in many ways. Mountains of yearly rate case testimony were combed and examined by lawyers and accountants at the level of infinitesimal detail. Hand-picked witnesses—insiders and outsiders—were thoroughly briefed to testify before the state and federal commissioners. And a considerable amount of top management time was spent in deliberations on the political circumstances surrounding rate hearings.

In another quarter, attention was simultaneously focused on the development of new technologies and their implementation

---

STRATEGIC CHANGE

Strategic Component	Regulated Environment	Competitive Environment
General Strategic Orientation	• Strategies driven by regulatory and technological considerations	• Strategies driven by market opportunities and financial needs

FIGURE 14

throughout the nationwide network. Bell Labs' basic research was
handsomely funded in the conviction that such support would pay
off in scientific advancement and technological superiority. Seven
Nobel Prize winners and a dazzling stream of patents at Bell Labs, as
well as constant productivity improvement in the operations of the
telecommunications system, attested to the rightness of that
conviction.

Under regulation, then, management's strategic orientation tilted
more toward these two areas—regulatory matters and technological
advance—than to new and existing markets or financial factors. This
is not to say the latter were neglected; indeed, they received increasing attention in recent years. It is simply to say that the Bell System's
historic focus was oriented—and appropriately so—toward its bread-
winners: regulatory relief and technological progress.

In the emerging competitive arena, the balance of management
attention began to shift. Even after divestiture, of course, AT&T continued to pay significant attention to the regulatory realities, and did
not diminish its attention to technological innovation. But its overall
strategic orientation moved sharply toward a stronger financial and
marketing emphasis. It was a shift of major proportions. Starting at
the top levels of the firm, it created a ripple effect down through the
sectors and lines of business, changing in the very fundamentals the
way the business was run. In sum, all parts of the management infrastructure had to change to reflect the redeployment of resources to
the new, strategic salients.

THE PLANNING PROCESS

Historically, AT&T's planning process was essentially a bottom-up
scheme (see Figure 15). Subsidiary units were required annually to
submit 5-year plans featuring capital and budgeting projections.
Those projections were derived from estimates of demand for local
and long distance service and for customer equipment. Capital needs
for each subsidiary were provided by AT&T after a thorough review
of the "construction program." This was an exhaustive process
whereby the merits of each program were examined using time-
tested engineering economics. With a few exceptions (notably
Pacific Tel in the late 1970s) capital dollars would be made available
for each approved project if future earnings for that subsidiary
appeared satisfactory. Where internally generated funds were not

STRATEGIC CHANGE

Strategic Component	Regulated Environment	Competitive Environment
Planning Process	• Plans derived mostly from below • Construction program oriented	• Tied more to top-down strategy • Cash flow oriented

FIGURE 15

available, AT&T would raise the money externally through debt or equity offerings.

The process was based on a well-tested faith that regulatory commissions would allow sufficient earnings to be raised to cover capital costs and provide a fair rate of return.

This was the essence of the planning system. It worked the way it was designed to work—attuned to AT&T's regulatory setting and to its obligation to provide universal, end-to-end service. By most measures it worked well, benefitting the customer, the shareholder, the employee, and the public at large. But it was possible only because the regulatory franchise, with its guarantee of market share, minimized the external threat from potential predators.

In the competitive mode, of course, this guarantee vanished. And so the planning process had to shift to a new orientation. Strategies could no longer be derived from below through extrapolations from past demand; now they had to be coordinated from above and dictated by market conditions. In addition, financial constraints and cash flow needs had to play a more prominent role as the investment risk rose.

Soon after the decision to divest, therefore, a complete new business planning system, the Integrated Planning and Resource Allocation Process (IPRAP), was conceived and implemented. This early initiative allowed AT&T to move through the transition period with a new planning process up and running. It helped prepare the way for the many other changes to come.

FINANCIAL POLICIES

Financial policy and financial structure also had to undergo substantial change. Under heavy regulation there had been a strong predisposition toward dividends, as opposed to growth (see Figure 16). As deregulation proceeded, however, the "widows and orphans" stock began to change its image. While steady dividend performance remained an objective, pressures for growth were increasing steadily.

A less visible but equally important aspect of financial policy involved capital recovery strategies. In an era when market share was reasonably secure, the corporation could focus on highly reliable products with long life cycles. Depreciation schedules, accordingly, were stretched over long periods of time and were closely controlled by the FCC and state commissions.

In the free-for-all postdivestiture atmosphere, however, new market entrants could "niche" the more profitable products and service areas with variable quality lines, leaving AT&T with excess inventory or obsolescence.

AT&T therefore pushed the regulators for shorter depreciation schedules that would provide funds to help quicken product introduction and reduce reliance on external funding. These policies, in

STRATEGIC CHANGE

Strategic Component	Regulated Environment	Competitive Environment
Financial Policies	• Predisposition toward dividends	• Predisposition toward growth of stock
	• Long capital recovery schedules	• Short capital recovery schedules
	• Higher debt structure	• Lower or no debt structure
	• Heavy external financing	• Mostly internally generated financing

FIGURE 16

fact, are still in the midst of change. Shortened depreciation schedules will lead to a gradual lowering of AT&T's debt, bringing it more in line with other companies with similar risk factors.

Such changes are far from trivial. They are fundamental differences in ways of doing business, even the ways of thinking about a business. Accordingly, the AT&T board of directors moved soon after divestiture to elect a highly experienced and repected outside financial authority, Bob Kavner, as chief financial officer, replacing the comptroller, Bob Flint, who was to retire. Flint was preeminent in his grasp of financial policy under regulation. Kavner brought with him the knowledge and viewpoint of the competitive context, much needed to lead the financial organization into its new mode of management.

TECHNOLOGY DEVELOPMENT

Bell Laboratories is world-renowned for its contributions to basic research. The emphasis on scientific innovation that gave rise to this performance was made possible by AT&T's size, its management's commitment, and the stability attendant on a regulated business environment. In the competitive arena it would appear reasonable to expect a shift of research focus toward the practical side—the application of the fruits of technological research. (See Figure 17.)

STRATEGIC CHANGE		
Strategic Component	**Regulated Environment**	**Competitive Environment**
Technology Development	• Emphasis on fruits of basic research	• Emphasis on application of mature technology
	• R&D driven by technological opportunity	• R&D driven by customer needs

FIGURE 17

Furthermore, insulated from the demands of a competitive marketplace, Bell Labs could more readily pursue avenues of technological opportunity (the results of which often coalesced in the interests of the nation) without concern for loss of market share. In the post-divestiture era, customer needs will undoubtedly find their way back through the product development process into the laboratories of research.

PRICING PHILOSOPHY

Still another strategic component to undergo profound change was pricing philosophy (see Figure 18). The traditional goal of universal service had called for cross-subsidies to keep local rates down so that virtually everyone could afford a phone. Now that competitive performance was the measure, however, each product and service would have to stand on its own, its price determined solely by costs, competitors' prices, and market strategy. Long-distance rates would have

STRATEGIC CHANGE

Strategic Component	Regulated Environment	Competitive Environment
Pricing Philosophy	• Subsidization of local service	• Each product or product line self-sufficient
	• Prices based on ''value of service''	• Prices based on costs, competitor's prices and market strategy
	• National price averaging for long-distance calls	• Route-by-route pricing
	• Comparative costs not relevant	• Goal is to be low-cost producer

FIGURE 18

to be recalculated using similar criteria, applied on a route-by-route basis instead of national averaging.

Managers unfamiliar with competitive pricing strategies had to learn completely new methodologies. Moreover, AT&T's accounting system was not designed to produce the cost data needed to price every widget with the new techniques. The entire accounting system had to be overhauled and redesigned—an immense task, but one absolutely necessary to survival in the postdivestiture world.

MARKET STRATEGY

At the center of all the changes so far discussed was the pivotal necessity to forge new market and product strategies (see Figure 19). The traditional Bell System had served relatively monolithic markets with broad product-line offerings. To continue such procedures, however, would now spell disaster. AT&T's numerous and vigorous competitors viewed the telecommunications market not as monolithic but as highly differentiated, with pockets of highly lucrative opportunities. Their aim was to skim the cream off the market by offering selected customers specialized, sophisticated products and services not available from AT&T.

The company had to move fast to respond. Markets were analyzed and segmented into various customer populations. Organizations were reconfigured to match the newly defined market sectors. Fur-

---

STRATEGIC CHANGE

Strategic Component	Regulated Environment	Competitive Environment
Market Strategy	• Monolithic markets	• Segmented markets
	• Standardized offerings	• Customized offerings
	• Demand expected	• Demand stimulated

FIGURE 19

ther, to meet the specific demands of specific segments, previously standardized products became more and more customized. A new phrase, "customer satisfaction," came to replace the words "universal service" in the parlance of managers up and down the line.

Beyond segmenting the existing markets, AT&T had to become more aggressive in seeking and creating new ones. Formerly, increases in demand had been taken for granted; Bell was the only game in town. Now the company had to stimulate that demand—or watch its competitors get there first.

PRODUCT STRATEGY

Product timing was another factor that took on more urgency (see Figure 20). In earlier days, when few rivals threatened to capture the assured base of customers, AT&T's watchwords had been high product reliability, long product life cycles, and superior efficiency. But in the unrestrained modern telecommunications marketplace, new product introductions proliferated. AT&T was forced to shorten the life cycles of its product lines to stay competitive.

It was a reorientation that permeated every aspect of the research-development-manufacturing-marketing-sales continuum. Many found the adjustments difficult to accept, involving as they did

---

STRATEGIC CHANGE

Strategic Component	Regulated Environment	Competitive Environment
Product Strategy	• Product timing not crucial	• Product timing critical
	• Long product life cycles	• Short product life cycles

FIGURE 20

a basic shift in values and standards. But all recognized that the changes were necessary to survival.

ORGANIZATIONAL ORIENTATION

The massive restructuring effort, already detailed, had as its essential feature the decentralization of AT&T's operations into market-segmented lines of business, each with substantial autonomy (see Figure 21). Corporate Headquarters was pared to one-tenth its former size and devoted to general corporate direction, overall policy, and strong financial control. It was not reorientation but transformation, requiring a complete redefinition of roles, relationships, and accountabilities.

STRATEGIC CHANGE

Strategic Component	Regulated Environment	Competitive Environment
Organizational Orientation	• Large/centralized	• Smaller/decentralized
	• Functional structures	• Market segmented structures
	• Geographic operational profit centers	• Market/product line of business profit centers

FIGURE 21

CORPORATE CULTURE

The subject of corporate culture, as well, has been treated in a prior chapter that explored why and how the corporate belief system had to change (see Figure 22). The move from a consensus-oriented sys-

STRATEGIC CHANGE

Strategic Component	Regulated Environment	Competitive Environment
Corporate Culture	• Consensus oriented	• Risk oriented
	• Regulatory ''mindset''	• Marketplace ''mindset''
	• Reward system: slow steady progression for majority of employees	• Reward system: weighted more to individual performance. Large differences in salary treatment
	• Bias toward deliberation	• Bias toward action

FIGURE 22

tem of management to a more individualistic, risk-oriented one was discussed. Also outlined were the pervasive changes in reward system, the basis for promotions, salary increases, personal recognition, and so on.

SUMMARY

A review of Figure 23, a schematic presentation of the strategic components discussed above, will confirm that while all nine can be viewed separately, they are interrelated and interdependent. In the aggregate, they demonstrate a massive corporate reorientation, of such magnitude as to affect virtually every employee and every job. An entire coherent system of management had to undergo a transformation of extraordinary proportions.

But the transformation was no more radical than was the change in the business environment—the replacement of regulation by competition. It was a change rooted in national policy shifts and sealed by divestiture. For AT&T, the pace of change might abate with time. But there would never be a return to the steady-state existence of the former Bell System.

From Regulation to Competition: How Strategic Components Change the AT&T Case		
Strategic Component	Historic Regulated Environment	Emerging Competitive Environment
General Strategic Orientation	• Strategies driven by regulatory and technological considerations	• Strategies driven by market opportunities and financial needs
Planning Process	• Plans derived mostly from below • Construction program oriented	• Tied more to top-down strategy • Cash flow oriented
Financial Policies	• Predisposition toward dividends • Long capital recovery schedules • Higher debt structure • Heavy external financing	• Predisposition toward growth of stock • Short capital recovery schedules • Lower or no debt structure • Mostly internally generated financing
Technology Development	• Emphasis on fruits of basic research • R&D driven by technological opportunity	• Emphasis on application of mature technology • R&D driven by customer needs
Pricing Philosophy	• Subsidization of local service • Prices based on "value of service" • National price averaging for long-distance calls • Comparative costs not relevant	• Each product line self-sufficient • Prices based on cost, competitor's prices and market strategy • Route-by-route pricing • Goal is to be low-cost producer
Market Strategy	• Monolithic markets • Standardized offerings • Demand expected	• Segmented markets • Customized offerings • Demand stimulated
Product Strategy	• Product timing not crucial • Long product life cycles	• Product timing critical • Short product life cycles
Organizational Orientation	• Large/centralized • Functional structures • Geographic operational profit centers	• Smaller/decentralized • Market segmented structures • Market/product line of business profit centers
Corporate Culture	• Consensus oriented • Regulatory "mindset" • Reward system: slow, steady progression for majority of employees • Bias toward deliberation	• Risk oriented • Marketplace "mindset" • Reward system: weighted more to individual performance. Large differences in salary treatment • Bias toward action

FIGURE 23

POSTDIVESTITURE: A TASTE OF THINGS TO COME

It was not long after January 1, 1984—Divestiture Day—that the results of these strategic shifts began to become evident. Scores of new products were announced. Joint ventures with foreign firms were executed. A number of petitions exhorted the FCC to free AT&T

of remaining structural constraints and to change capital reuse schedules for capital recovery. No less important, focused efforts were initiated to redefine corporate missions and reshape the culture.

How far and how fast AT&T can adapt remains to be seen. There is no doubt, however, that the company will continue to evolve and define its new strategic identity in the years to come. The process will merit close attention. For the full evolution from a stable, regulated business to a highly competitive venture is not often enacted on such a large and dramatic scale.

In sum, AT&T's experience has demonstrated, and will continue to demonstrate, the stark and profound differences between the two modes of management. It may serve therefore as a useful example for other industries facing the prospect of deregulation.

Chapter 7

Crucial Questions for the Future

By mid-1984, just one half year after divestiture, business scholars and historians have already begun the process of assessment that will surely continue for years to come. Unquestionably, they will examine the broad economic, political, and technological forces that coalesced in the government mandate. Others, particularly the media and the public, will focus on the shorter-term issues of cost, price, and service impact following divestiture.

Many, both inside and outside the company, are pondering the extraordinary fact that despite decades of telecommunications excellence unequalled anywhere in the world, despite the strength of the argument for unified management of the nation's telephone network, despite strenuous objections from opinion leaders and serious concerns expressed by other sectors of the federal government itself, the Justice Department waged its perennial battle to break up the Bell System . . . and won. The unpersuaded or unsatisfied will continue to ask, Why? In whose interest was the effort pressed? And, having won, were the goals of divestiture achieved?

Certainly it is not within the scope of this book to answer comprehensively such questions. Indeed, it may be a long time before a definitive pattern of answers begins to emerge. Media reaction offered nothing but conflicting testimony: "For the consumer, costs will go up and service down . . . prepare for deteriorating service," *Forbes* warned on the day after divestiture, "We'll profit from a revamping of the system . . . the world's best telephone system could become even better," asserted *Time* on November 21, 1983, no less authoritatively. Accurate judgments as to the long-term effects will have to wait, it seems, for the clarity of historical perspective.

It is the fervent hope of the writer that during this necessary passage of time the crucial questions surrounding divestiture do not become obscured or obfuscated—particularly those regarding the circumstances leading to the signing of the agreement. For the ability to draw sound and useful lessons from the divestiture experience will surely depend as much on the quality and aptness of the questions asked as on the analytical powers brought to bear upon them.

It is in that spirit that the following questions are briefly discussed—not as an exhaustive list, but as a few of the many potentially fruitful lines of inquiry that might be pursued in future years.

PRIME MOVERS

Who were the moving forces—collectively and individually—behind the deregulation and break-up of the Bell System?

As discussed in Chapter 1, the tributary factors converging in divestiture were complex and diverse—so much so that a great deal remains to be understood about the roles of the protagonists and the interests represented. Why, for example, was the Justice Department so devoted to the cause?

Were size and power really the issue, in light of the extraordinary quality of service provided, its low cost, and the pervasive regulation to which it was subject? Perhaps a retrospective analysis of the voluminous antitrust testimony of both sides would help to clarify some of the more obscure aspects of such unsettled questions.

And what of Judge Greene's role, during the progress of the trial, in suggesting AT&T's guilt on several counts? And of his statement that although decades of AT&T management had acted in the public interest, the *potential* for abuse of power existed for future generations of management? Was this, in effect, a judgment of guilt prospectively as well?

As for the regulatory forces, was not the FCC's effort to deregulate the industry in an orderly fashion proceeding on course? Well before the MFJ was concluded, AT&T had agreed to form a separate subsidiary to market and sell home and office equipment in an open, competitive marketplace. Further, moves preliminary to detariffing long distance had already begun. Would not this gradual introduction of competition over time have answered concerns regarding monopoly power? While no one can ever be certain of untravelled paths, such questions should prove highly relevant to future analysis.

Of course, no assessment should omit the role of the U.S. Congress in the predivestiture context. During the turbulent years of the 1970s, the legislative branch was the one body that could have exercised a guiding influence on the overall direction of telecommunications policy. It had, after all, set the goals and standards that had proved so durable in the preceding half-century. Yet year after year, beginning with the Consumer Communications Reform Act of 1976, attempts to arrive at a new and equitable legislative mandate consistently ended in failure.

Why? Why was Congress unable to take the lead in making new policy? What were the political interests at stake among the members of Congress—especially among key members of the relevant congressional committees?

On a broader level, what is the role of the legislature in this arena? Should it establish policy guidelines and national priorities? Or should it stand aside and let regulatory trends, judicial proceedings, and market forces set the course?

Among various questions seldom asked is, Where was the executive branch? Although concern regarding the impact of the Bell System's dissolution was heard from various quarters in and out of government, the executive did not choose to intervene. Did it underestimate that impact, or did its "neutrality" reflect an unequivocal, ideological position on the part of the incumbent administration? Did silence convey consent?

Additionally, and significantly, what did technology contribute as an agent of change? Proponents of divestiture argue that the advancement and merging of communications and computer technology fostered the inevitability of competition within the industry and were influential in the breakup of the Bell System. Opponents pointed to the prolific record of Bell Laboratories innovations and argued that new technologies could continue to stream forth effectively—perhaps even more effectively—without such a radical transformation. Malcolm Schwartz, a witness from the consulting firm of Booz Allen Hamilton, warned during the trial that

> a less integrated structure with less resources to draw upon, and with different priorities, would neither fund fundamental research to the extent the Bell System had, nor would it have the ability to plan, design, and implement large-scale network-enhancing projects. As a result, there would be less technological growth and a less efficient network.

The "less integrated structure" is now an accomplished fact, but the questions remain. Would the preservation of network integration have allowed for more large-scale, coordinated deployment of new technologies in both long-distance and local-exchange segments, thus benefitting greater numbers of people? Under the competitive arrangement, will the "total network" concept be fragmented?

In short, did technology dictate competition and divestiture? Or did it simply present policymakers with a range of options?

An attendant inquiry might be addressed to the diminishing of Bell Laboratories as a national resource. As part of the traditional Bell System, Bell Labs was a unique organization in American life, combining a university-like capacity for basic research with an integral tie to a major industrial enterprise. Now, as part of the new AT&T, Bell Labs' role is being reassessed. Andrew Pollack of the *New York Times* expressed the concerns of many when he wrote, on January 1, 1984, that

> Bell Labs, no longer supported by telephone rate payers, might see its research funds shrink and its focus become more oriented toward short-term product development rather than the long-term research that has made it a national electronics resource.

Unquestionably, Bell Laboratories will remain a strong technological organization for some time to come. But whether AT&T will be able to afford its predivestiture level of expenditures as an act of faith in the fruits of research remains to be seen.

THE PROCESS

What governmental procedure best serves the public interest?

Of course, all the preceding questions build to one central, overarching inquiry. Was a courtroom trial the best way to formulate national telecommunications policy? In a *Telecommunications Policy* article in June 1983, Board Chairman Brown reflected on the years of turmoil:

> What do these developments suggest about the *process* by which public policy is made in the United States? Do the events which led to the dissolution of the Bell System reflect a triumph or a failure of our national policymaking apparatus? Is there not a more rational way to shape public policy for an industry that is such a critical part of the nation's social and economic infrastructure? Or is this a classic example of how changes take place in a free society?

Chapter 1's review of "The Context of Divestiture" presented a brief narrative of the governmental mandate Chairman Brown finds disturbing. It described how the Federal Communications Commission's course of deregulation gathered momentum without much public notice, while the national legislature remained paralyzed, unable to renew an industry charter. The decision to dismantle, meanwhile, emerged from an antitrust case whose very appropriateness was never accepted by the defendant and whose merits were debated even within the administration that prosecuted it.

Chairman Brown, therefore, raised a crucial question: Is there a better way within the governmental apparatus?

To go one step further, in a democratic society what is the role of "the public" itself in deciding a matter as important as telecommunications policy? During the years of national debate, all sides of course claimed to be acting "in the public interest." Moreover, all sides were often sincere in this. AT&T, certainly, was guided by an authentic, long-held belief in the public service ideals of universal service and network integration that were touchstones of its historic franchise. Advocates of the other side held that *they* were acting on behalf of the public in calling for an end of the regulated monopoly.

The peculiar fact, however, was that throughout the entire process the general public was not much heard from at all. Surveys showed that even after divestiture was announced few understood what the debate was about. And those who did know were not disposed to participate in it. Only after the breakup did the voice of the general public begin to be heard.

Why did this general unawareness of the political upheaval in the telephone industry exist? How could policymakers argue for years over the nature of the public interest with so little recourse to public opinion?

Put another way, why did the public choose to ignore the issue? In a time when the majority of telephone users would, if asked, have deemed their service highly satisfactory, why did they not defend the Bell System when it was under siege? Perhaps the comments by political analyst Richard Reeves, writing in *The New York Times Magazine* in February 1984, provide a clue:

> The energetic "politics of suspicion"—the suspicion on the part of the little guy that he is getting a raw deal from somebody or something big— has usually focused on "big business" as the enemy.

Was this a significant factor in the Bell System's demise? Was visceral resentment of "the big guy" indeed strong enough to offset the long experience of excellent and reliable service? While no way exists to measure such cultural mores, the questions are no less important in the effort to understand the public interest aspects of the issue.

AT&T'S DECISION

No doubt many pundits and Monday morning quarterbacks will have a heyday in assessing AT&T's decision to settle the case when it did, how it did. They will ask, for example, if the company took too long to accept the fact that a changed public mandate called for full-blown competition. Or, conversely, if it should have held out even longer.

In the same article cited above, Chairman Brown wrote of the decision to divest:

> We concluded that getting rid of the terrible uncertainty, and capitalizing on future market opportunities, were more important than vindicating our past behavior in a marketplace that no longer existed.

The power and momentum of the forces challenging the Bell System were formidable indeed. Moreover, as long as the trial went on, AT&T's long-term financial position could only decline, since competitors were rushing through ever-widening gates while the company itself was locked out of exploding new markets. Given the decade of effort to convey its view of the public interest, to no avail, and given its obligation to its shareowners to maintain financial vitality, AT&T's decision to divest when it did, as it did, can be viewed as the most judicious and timely one possible. It is my belief that in the fullness of time, AT&T's decision will be seen as precisely that.

CONCLUDING REMARKS

The many questions raised in this chapter might well leave the reader with a feeling of inconclusiveness—a sense that there are more questions than answers about divestiture. Indeed, this may be the case for some time—and some questions may never be adequately settled. As noted earlier, the purpose here is not to attempt *a priori* conclusions regarding the long-term consequences of divestiture, but rather to plead for care in formulating the questions surrounding the event, and to suggest some potential starting points for further lines of inquiry.

Having dwelt at some length on the history, management, and implementation of this monumental event, however, I feel a certain obligation to offer my personal, admittedly subjective, perspectives on the central issues: competition, divestiture, and the public interest.

Some of these perspectives may have already become evident. In brief, I believe that regulation in the telecommunications industry served the nation well for the better part of this century; that technological innovation, while calling for change, did not inexorably dictate full-scale competition, but only provided more choices for policymakers; that in fact the new technologies would have enabled competition to be introduced with increasing speed in selected arenas, particularly in home and office equipment and private-line services; that in any circumstances, the integrated nationwide network should have been preserved; that the government's charge of past or potential "abuse of size and power" was a hollow argument; that wise legislation could have been enacted to preserve the network and update regulatory powers, but that divestiture has all but precluded such legislative leadership; and, finally, that AT&T had no recourse but to protect its shareholders, its employees, and its customers by acceding to the government's order, since that order was the only available doorway to the promising new markets from which the company had been barred.

To summarize these observations: the public interest might have been better served by speeding up the regulatory process or by new legislation, either of which could have opened appropriate markets to competition and still have preserved the integrated design, operation, and maintenance of the network—thus providing unified service from customer to customer.

The irony of the government's divestiture mandate is that it undermined, in a way, the stated purpose of competition: to provide the customer with greater choice. It did so by destroying the one choice many customers appeared to want most: the choice of dealing with one telephone company for their total service needs. Customers now have *no* choice but to deal with different entities for the totality of premises equipment, local and long-distance calling, billing, and directory services. The fact that this highly valued choice no longer exists appears already to be making its way into the public consciousness—and arousing considerable dismay.

It is possible that competition will eventually yield benefits that will compensate—at least for some of the people, some of the time— for the loss of the integrated network and end-to-end service. It is possible that time will eventually heal all wounds and that a well-adjusted public will eventually find satisfaction in a voluntarily coordinated array of disparate companies. If, indeed, things turn out this way, then the end result will have been worth the employee traumas and customer dislocations of the divestiture transition.

In the meantime, however, I cannot escape a sense of the profound loss to the nation involved in the dismantling of the integrated network—nor can I escape the conviction that it is a loss that could have been avoided by more far-sighted public policymaking.

Chapter 8

A Final Reflection

The primary focus of this book has centered on *how* the divestiture was accomplished. Foregoing chapters have described the decision-making process of officers, the incremental development of implementation plans, and the formidable achievements of employees in carrying out those plans. A general picture has been sketched of both the magnitude and the intricacy of the task of divestiture.

Throughout these chapters, an implicit constant has been the central role played by employee motivation. It may, therefore, be fitting to conclude with some reflections on this intangible but essential quality. How did Bell Systems employees do it?

In the rich, recent literature of corporate culture, it is received wisdom that the success of any corporate venture depends greatly upon the degree to which employees are sincerely committed to that venture. Without such commitment, most analysts agree, even the most brilliant strategies will yield disappointing results.

It is interesting to consider divestiture in this context. As we have seen, tens of thousands of employees had to summon their deepest resources in the service of a goal that many—perhaps most—were far from committed to. And yet they rose to the call and responded with remarkable success.

Are there conclusions to be drawn from this admittedly exceptional case? Is "commitment" merely a currently fashionable catchword?

Obviously, it is more than that. Few experienced managers would deny the close relationship between employee commitment and the success of most business endeavors. However, the divestiture experience suggests that other ingredients—notably discipline, skill, and trust—are required for the accomplishment of large-scale and complex tasks. Indeed, it may have been a group of firmly committed but poorly disciplined employees who originally inspired the quip that "having lost their direction, they redoubled their efforts."

The Bell System, fortunately, had extraordinarily deep reserves of discipline, knowledge, and mutual trust to call upon in its ultimate crisis. And there were precedents in its history for marshaling such reserves in times of urgent need. Each year fires, storms, floods, or other natural disasters evoked heroic efforts on the part of individuals, work units, and sometimes nationally mobilized Bell teams to restore service quickly and efficiently. A constant reminder of this heritage was a picture hung in thousands of Bell System work areas. The painting memorializes the "Spirit of Service," symbolized by an installer in snowshoes, patrolling the Boston-to-New York toll line right through the swirling "blizzard of '88."

More relevant, if less dramatic, analogies to the divestiture challenge were the numerous "cutovers" to more and more advanced switching systems through the years—changes that had to be achieved under extreme time pressure to avoid service disruptions. Each of these cutovers was troubling, even distressing, to some employees, since each tended to involve the displacement of human beings by machines. Yet each was achieved with efficiency and care. The collective skill and discipline of Bell System people, their ability to coordinate thousands of activities and to operate smoothly in the crunch, enabled them not only to perform complex jobs within tight time frames but also to pursue objectives that were less than desirable for them personally. So when the Bell System work force confronted the greatest—and most objectionable—challenge in their history, they were well prepared for it.

Ultimately, then, one of the most striking lessons of divestiture may be the perspective it affords on the concept of employee commitment. The ostentatious displays of enthusiasm that sometimes pass for commitment may be less important, less authentic, than the existence of a long-term covenant of trust between the managers and the managed.

Bell executives had earned the trust and respect of their people over a long history of judicious decision making. When they made the decision that divestiture was the appropriate course—the mandate of a changed public policy—employee shock was tempered by a widespread and spontaneous assumption that the decision must be basically sound. This assumption enabled them to summon their energies in good faith, even if in low spirits. Furthermore, they knew their leadership trusted them to come through. And they were determined to live up to that trust.

Just as there may be no motivating force equal to the power of mutual trust, there may be no employee attribute more valuable than the habit of disciplined participation in a common cause. Even well-intentioned employees cannot succeed at complex, interdependent endeavors without a high level of skill and a tradition of team effort.

Thus, to the question, How did Bell people do it? we can answer that the Bell System's traditions equipped employees with a powerful legacy: a willingness to accept and abide by their leaders' decisions; a pride in their ability to carry out those decisions; a panoply of skills and a capacity for coordinated teamwork on a grand scale. Just the constellation of qualities needed for the job.

Nonetheless, no one who witnessed or took part in this high corporate drama could escape a sense that there was profound irony in the spectacle of the mighty army of Bell employees, whose devotion to the company was of an intensity rare in the modern corporate world, and whose careers had been devoted to the integration of the network, working diligently to pull it all apart. One respondent to the Corporate Culture Survey undoubtedly expressed the feelings of many when he described his reactions to divestiture:

It was like Greek theatre—a tragedy with a certain inevitability to it all, with a personal sense of involvement in events of historic proportions. . . .

Disappointment at the loss of the nobility of what was, and of the ties, friendships and symbols that bound us together as one system. . . .

Pride . . . at having been part of an institution that lasted for a hundred years and that changed the face of our nation and society for the better. . . .

> Involvement . . . in the sense of personal participation in the begin-
> nings of two of the most potentially powerful revolutions of mankind:
> micro-electronics and bio-genetics, one of which our technology cre-
> ated and the other which it enhanced.
>
> Relief in the sense that we recaptured through our pain much, if not
> all, of the freedom we need to shape our own destiny and that the time
> had come to look forward and put behind us the debilitating effects of
> continued and prolonged controversy and to share in the excitement
> of what now might be.

These days, with the trauma of divestiture behind them, former
Bell System people in all quarters are looking forward rather than
back. Their much-tested legacy of discipline, skill, and energy will
be put to the service of unfamiliar and constantly evolving new challenges. They will have to adopt new priorities, acquire new skills,
and selectively forget some of their old habits and received ideas.

But it is to be hoped that they do not forget what is enduring in
their uncommon and distinguished heritage. It is to be hoped that
they bring to the new missions the spirit with which they pursued
the old—that is, the aspiration to "change the face of society for the
better." If they do, the telecommunications future for the nation is
bright indeed.

Epilogue

The Lighter Side of Divestiture

Many a Truth Is Said in Jest

Americans have always tended to respond with humor when confronted by serious matters. As James Thurber explained, "Humor is the other side of tragedy. Humor is a serious thing . . . one of our greatest and earliest national resources."

The break-up of the Bell System offered seemingly endless opportunities for humor, as illustrated by the cartoons reproduced on the following pages. Taken from national publications, these are but a small sampling of good-natured public reaction to the "serious" matter of divestiture, as seen through the eyes of our graphic humorists.

"Then she began picking on the long-distance phone company I chose."
Drawing by Modell; © 1984 The New Yorker Magazine, Inc.

Drawing by D. Fradon; © 1983 The New Yorker Magazine, Inc.

"This is Willis Dunwoodie. His department is corporate feelings."

Drawing by Weber; © 1980 The New Yorker Magazine, Inc.

Reprinted with special permission of King Features Syndicate, Inc.

"*I'm temporarily short until A.T. & T. gets all straightened out.*"

Drawing by Stevenson; © 1983 The New Yorker Magazine, Inc.

"And if elected I will reunite the phone company!"

Drawing by Sauers; © 1984 The New Yorker Magazine, Inc.

Berry's World

3-8

"Remember, Comrade, people who are willing to destroy an efficient telephone system may not be playing with a full deck."

"*Your Majesty, according to our study the shoe was lost for want of a nail,
the horse was lost for want of a shoe, and the rider was lost for want of a horse,
but the <u>kingdom</u> was lost because of overregulation.*"

Drawing by Dana Fradon; © 1980 The New Yorker Magazine, Inc.

Appendix

Modification of Final Judgment

UNITED STATES DISTRICT COURT FOR THE DISTRICT OF COLUMBIA

UNITED STATES OF AMERICA,	Plaintiff,	Civil Action
v.		No. 82-0192
WESTERN ELECTRIC COMPANY, INCORPORATED,		
AND AMERICAN TELEPHONE AND TELEGRAPH COMPANY,	Defendants.	

MODIFICATION OF FINAL JUDGMENT

Plaintiff, United States of America, having filed its complaint herein on January 14, 1949; the defendants having appeared and filed their answer to such complaint denying the substantive allegations thereof; the parties, by their attorneys, having severally consented to a Final Judgment which was entered by the Court on January 24, 1956, and the parties having subsequently agreed that modification of such Final Judgment is required by the technological, economic and regulatory changes which have occurred since the entry of such Final Judgment;

Upon joint motion of the parties and after hearing by the Court, it is hereby ORDERED, ADJUDGED, AND DECREED that the Final Judgment entered on January 24, 1956, is hereby vacated in its entirety and replaced by the following items and provisions:

I
AT&T
Reorganization

A. Not later than six months after the effective date of this Modification of Final Judgment, defendant AT&T shall submit to the Department of Justice for its approval, and thereafter implement, a plan of reorganization. Such plan shall provide for the completion, within 18 months after the effective date of this Modification of Final Judgment, of the following steps:

1. The transfer from AT&T and its affiliates to the BOCs, or to a new entity subsequently to be separated from AT&T and to be owned by the BOCs, of sufficient facilities, personnel, systems, and rights to technical information to permit the BOCs to perform, independently of AT&T, exchange telecommunications and exchange access functions, including the procurement for, and engineering, marketing and management of, those functions, and sufficient to enable the BOCs to meet the equal exchange access requirements of Appendix B;

2. The separation within the BOCs of all facilities, personnel and books of account between those relating to the exchange telecommunications or exchange access functions and those relating to other functions (including the provision of interexchange switching and transmission and the provision of customer premises equipment to the public); provided that there shall be no joint ownership of facilities, but appropriate provision may be made for sharing, through leasing or otherwise, of multifunction facilities so long as the separated portion of each BOC is ensured control over the exchange telecommunications and exchange access functions;

3. The termination of the License Contracts between AT&T and the BOCs and other subsidiaries and the Standard Supply Contract between Western Electric and the BOCs and other subsidiaries; and

4. The transfer of ownership of the separated portions of the BOCs providing local exchange and exchange access services from AT&T by means of a spin-off of stock of the separated BOCs to the shareholders of AT&T, or by other disposition; provided that nothing in this Modification of Final Judgment shall require or prohibit the consolidation of the ownership of the BOCs into any particular number of entities.

B. Notwithstanding separation of ownership, the BOCs may support and share the costs of a centralized organization for the provision of engineering, administrative and other services which can most efficiently be provided on a centralized basis. The BOCs shall provide, through a centralized organization, a single point of contact for coordination of BOCs to meet the requirements of national security and emergency preparedness.

C. Until September 1, 1987, AT&T, Western Electric, and the Bell Telephone Laboratories, shall, upon order of any BOC, provide on a priority basis all research, development, manufacturing, and other support services to enable the BOCs to fulfill the requirements of this Modification of Final Judgment. AT&T and its affiliates shall take no action that interferes with the BOCs' requirements of nondiscrimination established by section II.

D. After the reorganization specified in paragraph I(A)(4), AT&T shall not acquire the stock or assets of any BOC.

II
BOC
Requirements

A. Subject to Appendix B, each BOC shall provide to all interexchange carriers and information service providers exchange access, information access, and exchange services for such access on an unbundled, tariffed basis, that is equal in type, quality, and price to that provided to AT&T and its affiliates.

B. No BOC shall discriminate between AT&T and its affiliates and their products and services and other persons and their products and services in the:
1. procurement of products and services;
2. establishment and dissemination of technical information and procurement and interconnection standards;
3. interconnection and use of the BOC's telecommunications service and facilities or in the charges for each element of service; and
4. provision of new services and the planning for and implementation of the construction or modification of facilities, used to provide exchange access and information access.

C. Within six months after the reorganization specified in paragraph I(A)4, each BOC shall submit to the Department of Justice procedures for ensuring compliance with the requirements of paragraph B.

D. After completion of the reorganization specified in section I, no BOC shall, directly or through any affiliated enterprise:
1. provide interexchange telecommunications services or information services;
2. manufacture or provide telecommunications products or customer premises equipment (except for provision of customer premises equipment for emergency services); or
3. provide any other product or service, except exchange telecommunications and exchange access service, that is not a natural monopoly service actually regulated by tariff.

III
Applicability
and Effect

The provisions of this Modification of Final Judgment, applicable to each defendant and each BOC, shall be binding upon said defendants and BOCs, their affiliates, successors and assigns, officers, agents, servants, employees, and attorneys, and upon those persons in active concert or participation with each defendant and BOC who receive actual notice of this Modification of Final Judgment by personal service or otherwise. Each defendant and each person bound by the prior sentence shall cooperate in ensuring that the provisions of this Modification of Final Judgment are carried out. Neither this Modification of Final Judgment nor any of its terms or provisions shall constitute any evidence against, an admission by, or an estoppel against any party or BOC. The effective date of this Modification of Final Judgment shall be the date upon which it is entered.

IV
Definitions

For the purposes of this Modification of Final Judgment:

A. "Affiliate" means any organization or entity, including defendant Western Electric Company, Incorporated, and Bell Telephone Laboratories, Incorporated, that is under direct or indirect common ownership with or control by AT&T or is owned or controlled by another affiliate. For the purposes of this paragraph, the terms "ownership" and "owned" mean a direct or indirect equity interest (or the equivalent thereof) of more than fifty (50) percent of an entity. "Subsidiary" means any organization or entity in which AT&T has stock ownership, whether or not controlled by AT&T.

B. "AT&T" shall mean defendant American Telephone and Telegraph Company and its affiliates.

C. "Bell Operating Companies" and "BOCs" mean the corporations listed in Appendix A attached to this Modification of Final Judgment and any entity directly or indirectly owned or controlled by a BOC or affiliated through substantial common ownership.

D. "Carrier" means any person deemed a carrier under the Communications Act of 1934 or amendments thereto, or, with respect to intrastate telecommunications, under the laws of any State.

E. "Customer premises equipment" means equipment employed on the premises of a person (other than a carrier) to originate, route, or terminate telecommunications, but does not include equipment used to multiplex, maintain, or terminate access lines.

F. "Exchange access" means the provision of exchange services for the purpose of originating or terminating interexchange telecommunications. Exchange access services include any activity or function performed by a BOC in connection with the origination or termination of interexchange telecommunications, including but not limited to, the provision of network control signalling, answer supervision, automatic calling number identification, carrier access codes, directory services, testing and maintenance of facilities and the provision of information necessary to bill customers. Such services shall be provided by facilities in an exchange area for the transmission, switching, or routing, within the exchange area, of interexchange traffic originating or terminating within the exchange area, and shall include switching traffic within the exchange area above the end office and delivery and receipt of such traffic at a point or points within an exchange area designated by an interexchange carrier for the connection of its facilities with those of the BOC. Such connections, at the option of the interexchange carrier, shall deliver traffic with signal quality and characteristics equal to that provided similar traffic of AT&T, including equal probability of blocking, based on reasonable traffic estimates supplied by each interexchange carrier. Exchange services for exchange access shall not include the performance by any BOC of interexchange traffic routing for any interexchange carrier. In the reorganization specified in section I, trunks used to transmit AT&T's traffic between end offices and class 4 switches shall be exchange access facilities to be owned by the BOCs.

G. "Exchange area," or "exchange" means a geographic area established by a BOC in accordance with the following criteria:

    1. any such area shall encompass one or more contiguous local exchange areas serving common social, economic, and other purposes, even where such configuration transcends municipal or other local governmental boundaries;

    2. every point served by a BOC within a State shall be included within an exchange area;

    3. no such area which includes part or all of one standard metropolitan statistical area (or a consolidated statistical area, in the case of densely populated States) shall include a substantial part of any other standard metropolitan statistical area (or a consolidated statistical area, in the case of densely populated States), unless the Court shall otherwise allow; and

    4. except with approval of the Court, no exchange area located in one State shall include any point located within another State.

H. "Information" means knowledge or intelligence represented by any form of writing, signs, signals, pictures, sounds, or other symbols.

I. "Information access" means the provision of specialized exchange telecommunications services by a BOC in an exchange area in connection with the origination, termination, transmission, switching, forwarding or routing of telecommunications traffic to or from the facilities of a provider of information services. Such specialized exchange telecommunications services include, where necessary, the provision of network control signalling, answer supervision, automatic calling number identification, carrier access codes, testing and maintenance of facilities, and the provision of information necessary to bill customers.

J. "Information service" means the offering of a capability for generating, acquiring, storing, transforming, processing, retrieving, utilizing, or making available information which may be conveyed via telecommunications, except that such service does not include any use of any such capability for the management, control, or operation of a telecommunications system or the management of a telecommunications service.

K. "Interexchange telecommunications" means telecommunications between a point or points located in one exchange telecommunications area and a point or points located in one or more other exchange areas or a point outside an exchange area.

L. "Technical information" means intellectual property of all types, including, without limitation, patents, copyrights, and trade secrets, relating to planning documents, designs, specifications, standards, and practices and procedures, including employee training.

N. "Telecommunications equipment" means equipment, other than customer premises equipment, used by a carrier to provide telecommunications services.

O. "Telecommunications" means the transmission, between or among points specified by the user, of information of the user's choosing, without change in the form or content of the information as sent and received, by means of electromagnetic transmission, with or without benefit of any closed transmission medium, including all instrumentalities, facilities, apparatus, and services (including the collection, storage, forwarding, switching, and delivery of such information) essential to such transmission.

P. "Telecommunications service" means the offering for hire of telecommunications facilities, or of telecommunications by means of such facilities.

Q. "Transmission facilities" means equipment (including without limitation wire, cable, microwave, satellite, and fibre-optics) that transmit information by electromagnetic means or which directly support such transmission, but does not include customer premises equipment.

V
Compliance Provisions

The defendants, each BOC, and affiliated entities are ordered and directed to advise their officers and other management personnel with significant responsibility for matters addressed in this Modification of Final Judgment of their obligations hereunder. Each BOC shall undertake the following with respect to each such officer or management employee:

1. The distribution to them of a written directive setting forth their employer's policy regarding compliance with the Sherman Act and with this Modification of Final Judgment, with such directive to include:

(a) an admonition that non-compliance with such policy and this Modification of Final Judgment will result in appropriate disciplinary action determined by their employer and which may include dismissal; and

(b) advice that the BOCs' legal advisors are available at all reasonable times to confer with such persons regarding any compliance questions or problems;

2. The imposition of a requirement that each of them sign and submit to their employer a certificate in substantially the following form:

The undersigned hereby (1) acknowledges receipt of a copy of the 1982 *United States v. Western Electric*, Modification of Final Judgment and a written directive setting forth Company policy regarding compliance with the antitrust laws and with such Modification of Final Judgment, (2) represents that the undersigned has read such Modification of Final Judgment and directive and understands those provisions for which the undersigned has responsibility, (3) acknowledges that the undersigned has been advised and understands that non-compliance with such policy and Modification of Final Judgment will result in appropriate disciplinary measures determined by the Company and which may include dismissal, and (4) acknowledges that the undersigned has been advised and understands that non-compliance with the Modification of Final Judgment may also result in conviction for contempt of court and imprisonment and/or fine.

VI
Visitorial Provisions

A. For the purpose of determining or securing compliance with this Modification of Final Judgment, and subject to any legally recognized privilege, from time to time:

1. Upon written request of the Attorney General or of the Assistant Attorney General in charge of the Antitrust Division, and on reasonable notice to a defendant or after the reorganization specified in section I, a BOC, made to its principal office, duly authorized representatives of the Department of Justice shall be permitted access during office hours of such defendants or BOCs to depose or interview officers, employees, or agents, and inspect and copy all books, ledgers, accounts, correspondence, memoranda and other records and documents in the possession or under the control of such defendant, BOC, or subsidiary companies, who may have counsel present, relating to any matters contained in this Modification of Final Judgment; and

2. Upon the written request of the Attorney General or of the Assistant Attorney General in charge of the Antitrust Division made to a defendant's principal office or, after the reorganization specified in section I, a BOC, such defendant, or BOC, shall submit such written reports, under oath if requested, with respect to any of the matters contained in this Modification of Final Judgment as may be requested.

B. No information or documents obtained by the means provided in this section shall be divulged by any representative of the Department of Justice to any person other than a duly authorized representative of the Executive Branch of the United States or the Federal Communications Commission, except in the course of legal proceedings to which the United States is a party, or for the purpose of securing compliance with this Final Judgment, or as otherwise required by law.

C. If at the time information or documents are furnished by a defendant to a plaintiff, such defendant or BOC represents and identifies in writing the material in any such information or documents to which a claim of protection may be asserted under Rule 26(c) (7) of the Federal Rules of Civil Procedure, and said defendant or BOC marks each pertinent page of such material, "Subject to claim of protection under Rule 26(c) (7) of the Federal Rules of Civil Procedure," then 10 days' notice shall be given by plaintiff to such defendant or BOC prior to divulging such material in any legal proceeding (other than a grand jury proceeding) to which that defendant or BOC is not a party.

VII
Retention of Jurisdiction

Jurisdiction is retained by this Court for the purpose of enabling any of the parties to this Modification of Final Judgment, or, after the reorganization specified in section I, a BOC to apply to this Court at any time for such further orders or directions as may be necessary or appropriate for the construction or carrying out of this

Modification of Final Judgment, for the modification of any of the provisions hereof, for the enforcement of compliance herewith, and for the punishment of any violation hereof.

VIII
Modifications

A. Notwithstanding the provisions of section II(D)(2), the separated BOCs shall be permitted to provide, but not manufacture, customer premises equipment.

B. Notwithstanding the provisions of section II(D)(3), the separated BOCs shall be permitted to produce, publish, and distribute printed directories which contain advertisements and which list general product and business categories, the service or product providers under these categories, and their names, telephone numbers, and addresses.

Notwithstanding the provisions of sections I(A)(1), I(A)(2), I(A)(4), all facilities, personnel, systems, and rights to technical information owned by AT&T, its affiliates, or the BOCs which are necessary for the production, publication, and distribution of printed advertising directories shall be transferred to the separated BOCs.

C. The restrictions imposed upon the separated BOCs by virtue of section II(D) shall be removed upon a showing by the petitioning BOC that there is no substantial possibility that it could use its monopoly power to impede competition in the market it seeks to enter.

D. AT&T shall not engage in electronic publishing over its own transmission facilities. "Electronic publishing" means the provision of any information which AT&T or its affiliates has, or has caused to be, originated, authored, compiled, collected, or edited, or in which it has a direct or indirect financial or proprietary interest, and which is disseminated to an unaffiliated person through some electronic means.

Nothing in this provision precludes AT&T from offering electronic directory services that list general product and business categories, the service or product providers under these categories, and their names, telephone numbers, and addresses; or from providing the time, weather, and such other audio services as are being offered as of the date of the entry of the decree to the geographic areas of the country receiving those services as of that date.

Upon application of AT&T, this restriction shall be removed after seven years from the date of entry of the decree, unless the Court finds that competitive conditions clearly require its extension.

E. If a separated BOC provides billing services to AT&T pursuant to Appendix B(C)(2), it shall include upon the portion of the bill devoted to interexchange services the following legend:

> This portion of your bill is provided as a service to AT&T. There is no connection between this company and AT&T. You may choose another company for your long distance telephone calls while still receiving your local telephone service from this company.

F. Notwithstanding the provisions of Appendix B(C)(3), whenever, as permitted by the decree, a separated BOC fails to offer exchange access to an interexchange carrier that is equal in type and quality to that provided for the interexchange traffic of AT&T, the tariffs filed for such less-than-equal access shall reflect the lesser cost, if any, of such access as compared to the exchange access provided AT&T.

G. Facilities and other assets which serve both AT&T and one or more BOCs shall be transferred to the separated BOCs if the use made by such BOC or BOCs predominates over that of AT&T. Upon application by a party or a BOC, the Court may grant an exception to this requirement.

H. At the time of the transfer of ownership provided for in section I(A)(4), the separated BOCs shall have debt ratios of approximately forty-five percent (except for Pacific Telephone and Telegraph Company which shall have a debt ratio of approximately fifty percent), and the quality of the debt shall be representative of the average terms and conditions of the consolidated debt held by AT&T, its affiliates and the BOCs at that time. Upon application by a party or a BOC, the Court may grant an exception to this requirement.

I. The Court may act *sua sponte* to issue orders or directions for the construction or carrying out of this decree, for the enforcement of compliance therewith, and for the punishment of any violation thereof.

J. Notwithstanding the provisions of section I(A), the plan of reorganization shall not be implemented until approved by the Court as being consistent with the provisions and principles of the decree.

Entered this 24th day of August, 1982.

/s/ *Harold H. Greene*

Harold H. Greene
United States District Judge

APPENDIX A

Bell Telephone Company of Nevada
Illinois Bell Telephone Company
Indiana Bell Telephone Company, Incorporated
Michigan Bell Telephone Company
New England Telephone and Telegraph Company
New Jersey Bell Telephone Company
New York Telephone Company
Northwestern Bell Telephone Company
Pacific Northwest Bell Telephone Company
South Central Bell Telephone Company
Southern Bell Telephone and Telegraph Company
Southwestern Bell Telephone Company
The Bell Telephone Company of Pennsylvania
The Chesapeake and Potomac Telephone Company
The Chesapeake and Potomac Telephone Company of Maryland
The Chesapeake and Potomac Telephone Company of Virginia
The Chesapeake and Potomac Telephone Company of West Virginia
The Diamond State Telephone Company
The Mountain States Telephone and Telegraph Company
The Ohio Bell Telephone Company
The Pacific Telephone and Telegraph Company
Wisconsin Telephone Company

APPENDIX B
PHASED-IN BOC PROVISION OF EQUAL EXCHANGE ACCESS

A.   1. As part of its obligation to provide non-discriminatory access to interexchange carriers, no later than September 1, 1984, each BOC shall begin to offer to all interexchange carriers exchange access on an unbundled, tariffed basis, that is equal in type and quality to that provided for the interexchange telecommunications services of AT&T and its affiliates. No later than September 1, 1985, such equal access shall be offered through end offices of each BOC serving at least one-third of that BOC's exchange access lines and, upon bona fide request, every end office shall offer such access by September 1, 1986. Nothing in this Modification of Final Judgment shall be construed to permit a BOC to refuse to provide to any interexchange carrier or information service provider, upon bona fide request, exchange or information access superior or inferior in type or quality to that provided for AT&T's interexchange services or information services at charges reflecting the reduced or increased cost of such access.

2. (i) Notwithstanding paragraph (1), in those instances in which a BOC is providing exchange access for Message Telecommunications Service on the effective date of this Modification of Final Judgment through access codes that do not permit the designation of more than one interexchange carrier, then, in accordance with the schedule set out in paragraph (1), exchange access for additional carriers shall be provided through access codes containing the minimum number of digits necessary at the time access is sought to permit nationwide, multiple carrier designation for the number of interexchange carriers reasonably expected to require such designation in the immediate future.

(ii) Each BOC shall, in accordance with the schedule set out in paragraph (1), offer as a tariffed service exchange access that permits each subscriber automatically to route, without the use of access codes, all the subscriber's interexchange communications to the interexchange carrier of the customer's designation.

(iii) At such time as the national numbering area (area code) plan is revised to require the use of additional digits, each BOC shall provide exchange access to every interexchange carrier, including AT&T, through a uniform number of digits.

3. Notwithstanding paragraphs (1) and (2), with respect to access provided through an end office employing switches technologically antecedent to electronic, stored program control switches or those offices served by switches that characteristically serve fewer than 10,000 access lines, a BOC may not be required to provide equal access through a switch if, upon complaint being made to the Court, the BOC carries the burden of showing that for particular categories of services such access is not physically feasible except at costs that clearly outweigh potential benefits to users of telecommunications services. Any such denial of access under the preceding sentence shall be for the minimum divergence in access necessary, and for the minimum time necessary, to achieve such feasibility.

B. 1. The BOCs are ordered and directed to file, to become effective on the effective date of the reorganization described in paragraph I(A) (4), tariffs for the provision of exchange access including the provision by each BOC of exchange access for AT&T's interexchange telecommunications. Such tariffs shall provide unbundled schedules of charges for exchange access and shall not discriminate against any carrier or other customer. Such tariffs shall replace the division of revenues process used to allocate revenues to a BOC for exchange access provided for the interexchange telecommunications of BOCs or AT&T.

2. Each tariff for exchange access shall be filed on an unbundled basis specifying each type of service, element by element, and no tariff shall require an interexchange carrier to pay for types of exchange access that it does not utilize. The charges for each type of exchange access shall be cost justified and any differences in charges to carriers shall be cost justified on the basis of differences in services provided.

3. Notwithstanding the requirements of paragraph 2, from the date of reorganization specified in section I until September 1, 1991, the charges for delivery or receipt of traffic of the same type between end offices and facilities of interexchange carriers within an exchange area, or within reasonable subzones of an exchange area, shall be equal, per unit of traffic delivered or received, for all interexchange carriers; provided, that the facilities of any interexchange carrier within five miles of an AT&T class 4 switch shall, with respect to end offices served

by such class 4 switch, be considered to be in the same subzone as such class 4 switch.

4. Each BOC offering exchange access as part of a joint or through service shall offer to make exchange access available to all interexchange carriers on the same terms and conditions, and at the same charges, as are provided as part of a joint or through service, and no payment or consideration of any kind shall be retained by the BOC for the provision of exchange access under such joint or through service other than through tariffs filed pursuant to this paragraph.

C. **1.** Nothing in this Modification of Final Judgment shall be construed to require a BOC to allow joint ownership or use of its switches, or to require a BOC to allow co-location in its building of the equipment of other carriers. When a BOC uses facilities that (i) are employed to provide exchange telecommunications or exchange access or both, and (ii) are also used for the transmission or switching of interexchange telecommunications, then the costs of such latter use shall be allocated to the interexchange use and shall be excluded from the costs underlying the determination of charges for either of the former uses.

2. Nothing in this Modification of Final Judgment shall either require a BOC to bill customers for the interexchange services of any interexchange carrier or preclude a BOC from billing its customers for the interexchange services of any interexchange carrier it designates, provided that when a BOC does provide billing services to an interexchange carrier, the BOC may not discontinue local exchange service to any customer because of nonpayment of interexchange charges unless it offers to provide billing services to all interexchange carriers, and provided further that the BOC's cost of any such billing shall be included in its tariffed access charges to that interexchange carrier.

3. Whenever, as permitted by this Modification of Final Judgment, a BOC fails to offer exchange access to an interexchange carrier that is equal in type and quality to that provided for the interexchange traffic of AT&T, nothing in this Modification of Final Judgment shall prohibit the BOC from collecting reduced charges for such less-than-equal exchange access to reflect the lesser value of such exchange access to the interexchange carrier and its customers compared to the exchange access provided AT&T.

Index

217

About the Author

W. Brooke Tunstall served as corporate vice president, Organization and Management Systems, for the AT&T Company. He was director of divestiture planning and cochairman of the Restructure Implementation Board—a principal forum for managerial review of the overall divestiture process. Recently, he has turned his extensive experience in matters of corporate planning, organization design, and corporate culture to private consulting.

Tunstall is a well-known writer and speaker on management matters. Recently published articles include "Cultural Transition at AT&T" (*Sloan Management Review*, 1983) and "Rites of Passage" (*Bell Telephone Magazine*, 1983). A graduate in engineering from The Johns Hopkins University, Tunstall is a cofounder of the International Council on Organization and Management, a member (and past chairman) of the Conference Board Organization Planning Council, and a trustee of the Institute for the Future. Tunstall lives in Summit, New Jersey.